SEX WORSHIP AND SYMBOLISM

PLATE I
TAURIC DIANA

SEX WORSHIP AND SYMBOLISM

SANGER BROWN II., M.D.

WITH ILLUSTRATIONS

**Fredonia Books
Amsterdam, The Netherlands**

Sex Worship and Symbolism

by
Sanger Brown II

ISBN: 1-58963-597-3

Copyright © 2001 by Fredonia Books

Reprinted from the 1922 edition

Fredonia Books
Amsterdam, The Netherlands
http://www.fredoniabooks.com

All rights reserved, including the right to reproduce this book, or portions thereof, in any form.

In order to make original editions of historical works available to scholars at an economical price, this facsimile of the original edition of 1922 is reproduced from the best available copy and has been digitally enhanced to improve legibility, but the text remains unaltered to retain historical authenticity.

TO
MY WIFE
HELEN WILLISTON BROWN

PREFACE

THE greater part of the first three chapters of this book appeared in the *Journal of Abnormal Psychology*. This material is reprinted here by the kind permission of the Editor of that Journal. This part of the subject is chiefly historical and the data here given is accessible as indicated by the references throughout the text, although many of these books are difficult to secure or are out of print. For this historical material I am particularly indebted to the writings of Hargrave Jennings, Richard Payne Knight and Doctor Thomas Inman. Most of the reference matter coming under the general heading of Nature Worship was obtained from comparatively recent sources, such as the publications of the Bureau of American Ethnology, of the Smithsonian Institute, and certain publications of the American Museum of Natural History. Frazer's *Golden Bough* and other writings of J. G. Frazer on Anthropology furnished much valuable information. The writings

Preface

of special investigators, among others those of Spencer, and A. W. Howitt, on Primitive Australian Tribes, and W. H. R. Rivers on the Todas have been freely drawn upon. A number of other books and references have been made use of, as indicated throughout the text. I have found two books by Miss J. Harrison, *i. e.*, *Themis* and *Ancient Art and Ritual*, of great value in interpreting primitive ceremonies and primitive customs in general.

My main object has been to give the life history of a primitive motive in the development of the race, and to emphasize the dynamic significance of this motive. Later other motives may be dealt with in more detail if it is proved that both in normal and abnormal psychology we may best understand the mental development of the individual through our knowledge of the development of the race.

I wish to take this opportunity to express my appreciation of the assistance rendered me by my wife.

CONTENTS

CHAPTER		PAGE
	INTRODUCTION	11
I	SIMPLE SEX WORSHIP	13
II	SYMBOLISM	33
III	SUN MYTHS, MYSTERIES AND DECADENT SEX WORSHIP	69
IV	INTERPRETATIONS	97
	REFERENCES AND BIBLIOGRAPHY	137
	INDEX	143

ILLUSTRATIONS

Plate

I TAURIC DIANA ....Frontispiece

Facing Page

II MEDALS POSSESSED BY PAYNE KNIGHT   16

    Fig. 1 Urus in the act of butting against the egg of chaos

    Fig. 2 Bacchus represented as a bull with a human face

    Fig. 3 Venus represented as a cow

    Fig. 4 Horns as the emblem of power

    Fig. 5 Proserpine crowned with ears of corn as the Goddess of Fertility

III BRONZE STATUE OF CERES 26

IV SYSTRUM WITH VARIOUS MEDALS 36

    Fig. 1 Head of Apollo crowned with laurel and obelisk ending in a cross (male symbol)

    Fig. 2 Runic medal with head surrounded by obelisks or rays and head of Vulcan

    Fig. 3 Goat terminating in tail of fish to show generative power of water. Earth underneath fertilized by this union and above cornucopia result of this fertility

    Fig. 4 Egyptian Systrum

    Fig. 5 Goddess Hierapolis the thyrsis of Bacchus in one hand and the globe in the other

    Fig. 6 Vulcan's head with fire tongs similar to those in fig. 2

    Fig. 7 An effeminate representation of Apollo

    Fig. 8 Wolf as the symbol of the sun

V INDIAN TEMPLE 46

Illustrations

VI CELTIC TEMPLE AND GREEK MEDALS 56

    Fig. 1 Talisman square on Greek medal
    Fig. 2 Egyptian Talisman
    Fig. 3 Asterisk of the sun in center of square on Syracuse medal
    Fig. 4 Celtic Temple in Zeeland
    Fig. 5 Minerva with an elephant's skin on her head
    Fig. 6 Horns as symbol of power
    Fig. 7 Minerva represented in the Indian manner with the elephant skin over her helmet
    Fig. 8 Deity represented by an elephant bearing the torch (male symbol) in his trunk and the cornucopia (female symbol) in his tail
    Fig. 9 Horns of the bull placed on the head of the elephant
    Fig. 10 Jupiter with the moon on his head and the sun in his hand
    Fig. 11 Minerva holding spear

VII TEMPLE DEDICATED TO BACCHUS AT PUZZUOLI 66

    Fig. 1 (a) Holy of Holies
          (b) Showing distance below level of the ground
          (c) Drains and conduits for flooding temple
    Fig. 2 (a) Apartments of priests
          (b) Portico
          (c) Holy of Holies
    Fig. 3 Circular plan of temple

VIII ORNAMENT FROM PUZZOLI TEMPLE 76

    Fig. 1 Wolf devouring grapes as destructive power of sun
    Fig. 2 Deity crowned with laurel wreath

IX ORNAMENT FROM PUZZOLI TEMPLE 86

Illustrations

X	EGYPTIAN FIGURES AND ORNAMENTS	94
	Fig. 1 Columns like the lotus which Isis holds	
	Fig. 2 Isis holding the stem of the lotus surmounted by the seed vessel in one hand and the cross in the other	
	Fig. 3 Horns and ears of cow on head of Venus	
XI	EGYPTIAN FIGURES AND ORNAMENTS	106
	Fig. 1 Symbol of sun over bull	
	Fig. 2 Lotus flower design	
	Fig. 3 Young shoots of lotus just when they have burst seed vessel	
	Fig. 4 Sun over Taurine Bacchus	
	Fig. 5 Crowning of Taurine Bacchus with wreath of laurel	
	Fig. 6 Lotus seed vessel used as a capital	
	Fig. 7 Same seed vessel surrounded by leaves	
XII	THE LOTUS AND MEDALS OF MELITE	116
	Fig. 1 Flower, leaf, and seed vessel of the lotus	
	Fig. 2 Generative spirit with wings like Jewish Cherubim brooding over matter	
	Fig. 3 The crab as the symbol of the productive powers of the waters	
XIII	BACCHUS AND MEDALS OF CAMARINA AND SYRACUSE	126
	Fig. 1 Incubation of the vital spirit represented by a serpent wreathed around an egg	
	Fig. 2 Oriental symbol of sun (disc with wings)	
	Fig. 3 Sun fructifying the waters represented by swan	
	Fig. 4 Victory mounting chariot of sun	
	Fig. 5 Victory flying before chariot of sun	
	Fig. 6 Asterisk in place of victory	
	Fig. 7 The vine between the creating deity (Bacchus) and the destroying deity represented by the tiger	
XIV	STATUE OF A BULL IN THE PAGODA OF TANJORE	134

INTRODUCTION

OUR knowledge of religion receives contributions from every quarter; even the student of mental diseases finds information that is of service to the student of religion. The reverse is equally true: a knowledge of religion sheds light upon even the science of mental disorders.

In this short book, a psychiatrist seeks in the study of one aspect of religious practice—the worship of procreating power—to gain a clearer understanding of the forms taken by certain kinds of mental diseases. His theory is that we may expect diseased minds to reproduce, or return to expressions of desire customary and official in societies of lower culture. This is, as a matter of fact, less a theory than a statement of observed facts; of this, the reader of these pages, if familiar with certain mental disorders, may readily convince himself.

But Doctor Brown's intention is not merely, perhaps not primarily, to draw the attention

Introduction

of the Psychiatrist to a neglected source of information, he aims at something of wider import and addresses a wider public. His purpose is no less than the tracing of the history of that great motive of action, the sex passion, as it appears in religion and the interpretation of its significance. Those who come to this book without the preparation of the specialist will find it not only replete with novel and surprising facts, but will find these facts placed in such a relation to each other and to life in general, as to illuminate both religion and human nature. This important result is made possible by the point of view from which the author writes, the point of view of racial development which has proved its fertility in so many directions.

JAMES H. LEUBA.

SEX WORSHIP AND SYMBOLISM

SEX WORSHIP AND SYMBOLISM

CHAPTER I
SIMPLE SEX WORSHIP

PSYCHIATRY, during recent years, has found it to its advantage to turn to related sciences and allied branches of study for the explanation of a number of the peculiar symptoms of abnormal mental states. Of these related studies, none have been of greater value than those which throw light on the mental development of either the individual or the race. In primitive races we discover a number of inherent motives which are of interest from the standpoint of mental evolution. These motives are expressed in a very interesting symbolism. It is the duty of the psychiatrist to see to what extent these primitive motives operate uncon-

Sex Worship and Symbolism

sciously in abnormal mental conditions, and also to learn whether an insight into the symbolism of mental diseases may be gained, through comparison, by study of the symbolism of primitive races. In the following discussion one particular motive with its accompanying symbolism is dealt with.

A great many of the institutions and usages of our present day civilization originated at a very early period in the history of the race. Many of these usages are carried on in modified form century after century, after they have lost the meaning which they originally possessed; it must be remembered, however, that in primitive races they were of importance, and they arose because they served a useful end. From the study of these remnants of former days, we are able to learn the trends of thought which activated and inspired the minds of primitive people. When we clearly understand these motives, we may then judge the extent of their influence on our present day thought and tendencies.

It has only been during comparatively recent times that the importance of primitive beliefs

PLATE II
MEDALS POSSESSED BY PAYNE KNIGHT

Fig. 1 Urus in the act of butting against the egg of chaos.
Fig. 2 Bacchus represented as a bull with a human face.
Fig. 3 Venus represented as a cow.
Fig. 4 Horns as the emblems of power.
Fig. 5 Proserpine crowned with ears of corn as the Goddess of Fertility.

Simple Sex Worship

and practices, from the standpoint of mental evolution, has been appreciated. Formerly, primitive man was regarded merely as a curiosity, and not as an individual from whom anything of any value whatever was to be learned. But more recent studies have changed all this. In order to illustrate this matter of the evolution and development of the human mind we can very profitably quote from Sir J. G. Frazer:* "For by comparison with civilized man the savage represents an arrested or rather a retarded state of social development, and an examination of his customs and beliefs accordingly supplies the same sort of evidence of the evolution of the human mind that an examination of the embryo supplies of the evolution of the human body. To put it otherwise, a savage is to a civilized man as a child is to an adult; and just as a gradual growth of intelligence in a child corresponds to, and in a sense recapitulates, the gradual growth of intelligence in the species, so a study of savage society at various stages of evolution enables us to follow approximately,

* The Scope of Social Anthropology; Psyche's Task.

though of course not exactly, the road by which the ancestors of the higher races must have travelled in their progress upward through barbarism to civilization. In short, savagery is the primitive condition of mankind, and if we would understand what primitive man was we must know what the savage now is."

To properly interpret these beliefs and conduct, certain facts must be kept in mind. One is that with primitive races the group stands for the unit, and the individual has little if any personality distinct from the group. This social state gives rise to what is spoken of as collective thought, collective feeling, group action, etc. Miss J. Harrison* considers this conception a very important one in primitive religious development. All that the race expresses, all that it believes, is an expression of collective feeling. As a result of this group thought, feelings and beliefs are developed which are entertained by every individual of the community. These racial feelings become a part of the race itself; they are inseparable from it, and they find ex-

* Themis, Introduction Page XI.

pression in the loftiest of sentiments and the most earnest of religious beliefs.

Our study is not primarily concerned with religious development, but since early man's deepest feelings found expression in what later became a religion, it is necessary to search for racial motives in primitive religions. These feelings are in no way comparable to the conscious religious beliefs of later times, which were worked out in many instances by an ingenious priesthood. The period when group feeling predominated far antedated such civilizations as those of Egypt and later Greece, for example, in which very elaborate religious systems existed.

With primitive people these deeper feelings appear to arise unconsciously rather than consciously. Moreover, probably as a result of collective thought and feeling, motives and beliefs are developed and elaborated in a way quite beyond the mental capacity of any one individual of the community. Beliefs are formulated which have a grandeur of conception and a beauty of expression well worthy of admiration. The beauty and native vigor of some of the earlier myths are examples of this. They live in the tribe as traditions. No one person seems to have written them; in fact, they are added to, changed and improved until they represent the highest expression of national feelings. Gilbert Murray has indicated this in the *Rise of the Greek Epic*. He emphasizes that there is found an expression of racial feelings, built up from many sources. Such Sagas are not the property of any one individual. The feelings they express are associated with the unconscious of the race, if such a term is permissible. Gilbert Murray,* in interpreting this element in primitive literature states: "We have also, I suspect, a strange unanalyzed-vibration below the surface, an undercurrent of desires and fears, and passions, long slumbering yet eternally familiar, which have for thousands of years lain near the root of our most intimate emotions and been wrought into the fabric of our most magical dreams. How far in the past ages this stream may reach back I dare not even

* Hamlet and Orestes.

Simple Sex Worship

surmise; but it sometimes seems as if the power of stirring it or moving with it were one of the last secrets of genius."

The importance of the collective or group feeling has been emphasized as thereby one sees how a fundamental racial motive becomes an integral part of the mental life of each and every member of the group. In primitive life every individual contributes something to this motive and in turn receives something from it. It enters into the developing mind and becomes inseparably associated with it. In studying the evolution of these motives one is studying the evolution of the human mind.

The motive which we have undertaken to explain has to do with one of the most important of instincts, *i. e.*, that of reproduction. The feelings associated with this instinct were raised to the dignity of religion, and in this we have the worship of sex. This worship is to be regarded as an unconscious racial expression, the result of group or collective feeling, the dynamic significance of which, from a biological standpoint, will appear later.

Sex Worship and Symbolism

Before proceeding, it is desirable to make reference to some of our sources of information. There are plenty of books on the history of Egypt, the antiquities of India or on the interpretation of Oriental customs, which make scarcely any reference to the deification of sex. We have always been told, for example, that Bacchus was the god of the harvest and that the Greek Pan was the god of nature. We have not been told that these same gods were representations of the male generative attribute, and that they were worshipped as such; yet, anyone who has access to the statuettes or engravings of these various deities of antiquity, whether they be of Egypt, of India or of China, cannot fail to see that they were intended to represent generative attributes. On account of the incompleteness of many books which describe primitive races, a number of references are given throughout these pages, and some bibliographical references are added.

As will be presently indicated, we have evidence from a number of sources to show sex was at one time frankly and openly worshipped by the primitive races of mankind. This worship has been shown to be so general and so widespread, that it is to be regarded as part of the general evolution of the human mind; it seems to be indigenous with the race, rather than an isolated or exceptional circumstance.

The American Cyclopedia, under Phallic Worship, reads as follows: "In early ages the sexual emblems were adored as most sacred objects, and in the several polytheistic systems the act or principle of which the phallus was the type was represented by a deity to whom it was consecrated: in Egypt by Khem, in India by Siva, in Assyria by Vul, in primitive Greece by Pan, and later by Priapus, in Italy by Mutinus or Priapus, among the Teutonic and Scandinavian nations by Fricco, and in Spain by Hortanes. Phallic monuments and sculptured emblems are found in all parts of the world."

Rawlinson, in his history of Ancient Egypt, gives us the following description of Khem: "A full Egyptian idea of Khem can scarcely be presented to the modern reader, on account of the grossness of the forms under which it was exhibited. Some modern Egyptologists endeavor to excuse or palliate this grossness; but it seems scarcely possible that it should not have been accompanied by indelicacy of thought or that it should have failed to exercise a corrupting influence on life and morals. Khem, no doubt, represented to the initiated merely the generative power in nature, or that strange law by which living organisms, animal and vegetable, are enabled to reproduce their like. But who shall say in what exact light he represented himself to the vulgar, who had continually before their eyes the indecent figures under which the painters and sculptors portrayed him? As impure ideas and revolting practices clustered around the worship of Pan in Greece and later Rome, so it is more than probable that in the worship of Khem in Egypt were connected similar excesses. Besides his priapic or 'Ithyphallic' form, Khem's character was marked by the assignment to him of the goat as his symbol, and by his ordinary title *Ka-mutf*, 'The Bull of His Mother,' *i. e.*, of nature."

Simple Sex Worship

This paragraph clearly indicates that the sexual organs were worshipped under the form of Khem by the Egyptians. The writer, however, has fallen into a very common error in giving us to understand that this was a degraded form of worship; from numerous other sources it is readily shown that such is not the case.

The following lines, from *Ancient Sex Worship,* substantiate the above remarks, and at the same time, they show the incompletenees of the writings of many antiquarians. In this book we read: "Phallic emblems abounded at Heliopolis and Syria and many other places, even into modern times. The following unfolds marvelous proof to our point. A brother physician, writing to Dr. Inman, says: 'I was in Egypt last winter (1865-66), and there certainly are numerous figures of gods and kings on the walls of the temple at Thebes, depicted with the male genital erect. The great temple at Karnac is, in particular, full of such figures and the temple of Danclesa, likewise, although that is of much later date, and built merely in imitation of old Egyptian art.' " The writer further states that this shows how

Sex Worship and Symbolism

completely English Egyptologists have suppressed a portion of the facts in the histories which they have given to the world. With all our descriptions of the wonderful temple of Karnac, it is remarkable that all mention of its association with sex worship should be omitted by many writers.

A number of travellers in Africa, even in comparatively modern times, have observed evidences of sex worship among the primitive races of that continent. Captain Burton* speaks of this custom with the Dahome tribe. Small gods of clay are made in priapic attitudes before which the natives worship. The god is often made as if contemplating its sexual organs. Another traveler, a clergyman,† has described the same worship in this tribe. He has observed idols in priapic attitudes, rudely carved in wood, and others made of clay. On the lower Congo the same worship is described, where both male and female figures with disproportionate genital organs are used for purposes of worship. Phallic

* Quoted by H. M. Westropp, Primitive Symbolism.
† J. W. Wood. The Uncivilized Races.

PLATE III
BRONZE STATUE OF CERES

EBONY STATUE OF CERES

Simple Sex Worship

symbols and other offerings are made to these simple deities.

Definite examples of the sexual act having religious significance may be cited. Richard Payne Knight* quotes a passage from Captain Cook's voyages to one of the Southern Pacific Islands. The Missionaries of the expedition on this occasion assembled the members of the party for religious ceremonies in which the natives joined. The primitive natives observed the ceremony with great respect and then with due solemnity enacted their form of sacred worship. Quite to the astonishment of the white people, this ceremony consisted of the open performance of the sexual act by a young Indian man and woman. This was entirely a religious ceremony, and was fittingly respected by all the natives present.

Hargrave Jennings† describes the same custom in India. An Indian woman of designated caste and vocation is selected. Many incantations and

* The Symbolical Language of Ancient Art and Mythology.
† The Rosicrucians.

strange rites are gone through. A circle, or "Vacant Enchanted Place" is rendered pure by certain rites and sprinkled with wine. Then secret charms are whispered three times in the woman's ear. The sexual act is then consummated, and the whole procedure before the altar is distinctly a form of sacrifice and worship.

Hodder M. Westropp in *Primitive Symbolism* has indicated the countries in which sex worship has existed. He gives numerous instances in ancient Egypt, Assyria, Greece and Rome. In India, as well as in China and Japan, it forms the basis of early religions. This worship is described among the early races of Greece, Italy, Spain, Scandinavia, and among the Mexicans and Peruvians of America as well. In Borneo, Tasmania, and Australia phallic emblems have been found. Many other localities have been mentioned by this writer and one seems fairly justified in concluding that sex worship is regularly found at one time in the development of primitive races. We shall now pass to another form of this same worship, namely, sacred prostitution.

Simple Sex Worship

There is abundant evidence to show that there was a time in the centuries before Christ when prostitution was held as a most sacred vocation. We learn of this practice from many sources. It appears that temples in a number of ancient cities of the East, in Babylonia, Nineveh, Corinth and throughout India, were erected for the worship of certain deities. This worship consisted of the prostitution of women. The women were consecrated to the support of the temple. They were chosen in much the same way as the modern woman enters a sacred church order. The returns from their vocation went to the support of the deity and the temple. The children born of such a union were in no way held in disgrace, but on the contrary, they appeared to have formed a separate and rather superior class. We are told that this practice did not interfere with a woman's opportunities for subsequent marriage. In India the practice was very general at one time. The women were called the "Women of the Idol." Richard Payne Knight speaks of a thousand sacred prostitutes living in each of the temples at Eryx and Corinth.

Sex Worship and Symbolism

A custom which shows even more clearly that prostitution was held as a sacred duty to women was that in Babylonia every woman, of high rank or low, must at one time in her life prostitute herself to any stranger who offered money. In *Ancient Sex Worship* we read: "There was a temple in Babylonia where every female had to perform once in her life a (to us) strange act of religion, namely, prostitution with a stranger. The name of it was Bit-Shagatha, or 'The Temple,' the 'Place of Union.'" Moreover we learn that once a woman entered the temple for such a sacred act she could not leave until it was performed.

The above accounts deal exclusively in the sacrifice made by women to the deity of sex. Men did not escape this sacrifice and it appears that some inflicted upon themselves an even worse one. Frazer* tells us of this worship which was introduced from Assyria into Rome about two hundred years before Christ. It was the worship of Cybele and Attis. These deities were attended by emasculated priests and the

* Odonis, Attis and Osiris.

Simple Sex Worship

priests in oriental costume paraded Rome in religious ceremony.

On one occasion, namely, "the day of blood" in the Spring, the chief ceremony was held. This, among other things, consisted in fastening an effigy of the god to a pine tree, which was brought to the temple of the Goddess Cybele. A most spectacular dance about the effigy then occurred in which the priests slashed themselves with knives, the blood being offered as sacrifice. As the excitement increased the sexual nature of the ceremony became evident. To quote from Frazer: "For man after man, his veins throbbing with the music, his eyes fascinated by the sight of streaming blood, flung his garments from him, leaped forth with a shout, and seizing one of the swords which stood ready for the service, castrated himself on the spot. Then he ran through the city holding the bloody parts in his hands and threw them into one of the houses which he passed in his mad career."

We see that this act directly corresponds with the part played by the female. The female prostituted herself, and the male presented his generative powers to the deity. Both the sacred prostitutes and emasculated priests were held in religious veneration.

The above references are sufficient to show that a simple form of sex worship has been quite generally found. It becomes apparent as we proceed that the worship of sex not only plays a part, but a very prominent part, in the developing mind of man. In the frank and open form of this worship it is quite clear that we are dealing with a very simple type of mind. These primitive people exhibit many of the qualities of the child. They are quite without sex consciousness. Their motives are at once both simple and direct, and they are doubtless sincere. Much misunderstanding has arisen by judging such primitive people by the standards of our present day civilization. Sex worship, while it held sway, was probably quite as seriously entertained as many other beliefs; it only became degraded during a decadent age, when civilization had advanced beyond such simple conceptions of a deity, but had not evolved a satisfactory substitute.

SYMBOLISM

CHAPTER II

SYMBOLISM

AS civilization advanced, the deification of sex was no longer frank and open. It came to be carried on by means of symbolism. This symbolism was an effort on the part of its originators to express the worship of the generative attributes under disguise, often understood only by the priests or by those initiated into the religious mysteries. The mysteries so frequently referred to in the religions of antiquity are often some expression of sex worship.

Sexual symbolism was very general at one time and remains of it are found in most of the countries where any form of sex worship has existed. Such remains have been found in Egypt, Greece, Italy, India, China, Japan, and indeed in most countries the early history of which is known to man.

Sex Worship and Symbolism

One important kind of symbolism had to do with the *form* of the object deified. Thus, it appears that certain objects,—particularly upright objects,—stones, mounds, poles, trees, etc., were erected, or used as found in nature, as typifying the male generative organ. Likewise certain round oval objects, discs, certain fruits and certain natural caves, were worshipped as representing the female generative organ. (The yoni of India.)

We also find that certain *qualities of animal or vegetable* nature were equally venerated, not because of their form, but because they stood for some quality desirable in the generation of mankind. Thus we find that some animals—the bull because of its strength and aggressive nature, the snake, perhaps because of its form or of its tenacity of life,—were male representatives of phallic significance. Likewise the fish, the dolphin, and a number of other aquatic cretures came to be female representatives. This may be shown over and over again by reference to the antique emblems, coins, and engravings of many nations.

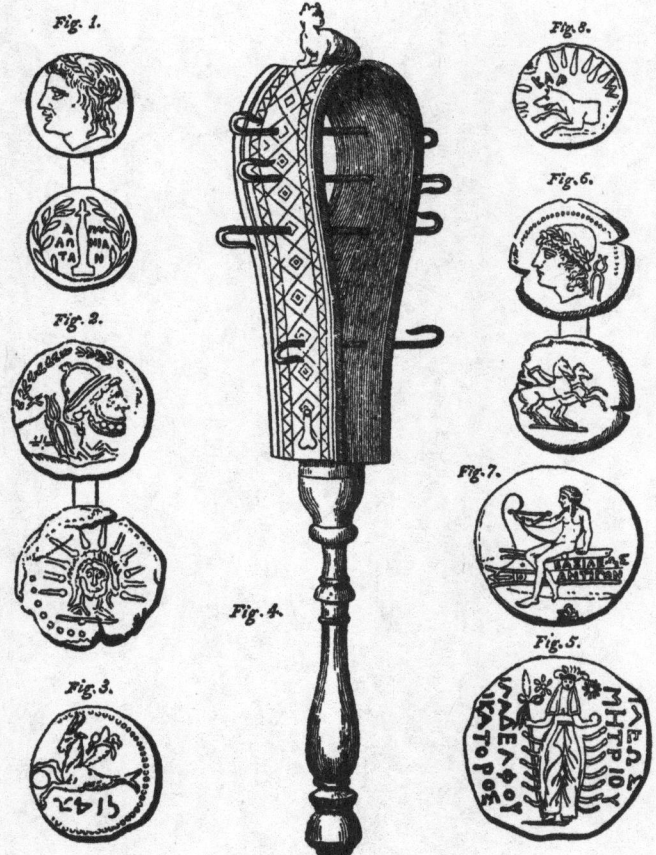

PLATE IV
SYSTRUM WITH VARIOUS MEDALS

Fig. 1 Head of Apollo crowned with laurel and obelisk ending in a cross (male symbol). 2 Runic medal with head surrounded by obelisks or rays and head of Vulcan. 3 Goat terminating in tail of fish to show generative power of water. Earth underneath fertilized by this union and above cornucopia result of this fertility. 4 Egyptian Systrum. 5 Goddess Hierapolis the thyrsis of Bacchus in one hand and the globe in the other. 6 Vulcan's head with fire tongs similar to those in fig. 2. 7 An effeminate representation of Apollo. 8 Wolf as the symbol of the sun.

Symbolism

Another later symbolism, which was adopted by certain philosophies, was more obscure but was none the less of distinct sexual significance. *Fire* is made to represent the male principle, and *water,* and much connected with it, the female. Thus we have Venus, born of the Sea, and accompanied by numerous fish representations. Fire worship was secondary to the universally found sun worship. The sun is everywhere the male principle, standing for the generative power in nature. At one time the symbolism is broad, and refers to generative nature in general. At another time it refers solely to the human generative organs. Thus, the Greek God Hermes, the God of Fecundity in nature, is at times represented in unmistakable priapic attitudes.

Still another symbolism was often used in India. This was the addition of a number of members to the deity, possibly a number of arms or heads. This was in order to express a number of qualities. Thus the deity was both generator and destroyer, one face showing benevolence and kindness, the other violence and rage. In many of the deities both male and female principles were represented in one,—an Androgyne deity—which was an ideal frequently attempted. The idea that these grotesque deities were merely the expression of eccentricity or caprice on the part of the originator is not to be entertained. Richard Payne Knight has pointed out that they occur almost entirely on national coins and emblems, and so were the expression of an established belief.

We shall refer first to the simpler symbols, those in which an object was deified because of its form.

It is perhaps not remarkable that *upright objects* should be selected because of their form as the simplest expression of phallic ideas. The simple upright for purposes of sex worship is universally found. An upright conical stone is frequently mentioned. Many of the stone idols or pillars, the worship of which was forbidden by the Bible, come under this group. Likewise, the obelisk, found not only in Egypt, but in modified forms in many other countries as well, embodies the same phallic principle. The usual

Symbolism

explanation of the obelisk is that it represented the rays of the sun striking the earth; when we speak of sun worship later, we shall see that this substantiates rather than refutes the phallic interpretation. The mounds of religious significance, found in many countries, were associated with sex worship. The Chinese pagodas are probably of phallic origin. Indeed, there is evidence to show that the spires of our Churches owe their existence to the uprights or obelisks outside the Temples of former ages. A large volume has been written by O'Brien to show that the Round Towers of Ireland (upright towers of prehistoric times) were erected as phallic emblems. Higgins, in the Anacalipsis, has amassed a great wealth of material with similar purport, and he shows that such "temples" as that of Stonehenge and others were also phallic. The stone idols of Mexico and Peru, the ancient pillar stones of Brittany, and in fact all similar upright objects, erected for religious purposes the world over, are placed in this same category. We shall presently give a number of references to show that the May-pole was associated with phallic worship and that it originated at a very remote period.

We shall now quote from some of the authors who have contributed to our knowledge of this form of symbolism, as thereby a clear idea of their meaning may be set forth. These interpretations are not generally advanced, and therefore we have added considerable corroborative evidence which we have been able to obtain from independent sources.

In an Essay on the Assyrian "Grove" and other Emblems, Mr. John Newton sums up the basis of this symbolism as follows: "As civilization advanced, the gross symbols of creative power were cast aside, and priestly ingenuity was taxed to the utmost in inventing a crowd of less obvious emblems, which should represent the ancient ideas in a decorous manner. The old belief was retained, but in a mysterious or sublimated form. As symbols of the male, or active element in creation, the sun, light, fire, a torch, the phallus or lingam, an erect serpent, a tall straight tree, especially the palm or fir or pine, were adopted. Equally useful for symbolism

Symbolism

were a tall upright stone (menhir), a cone, a pyramid, a thumb or finger pointed straight, a mask, a rod, a trident, a narrow bottle or amphora, a bow, an arrow, a lance, a horse, a bull, a lion, and many other animals conspicuous for masculine power. As symbols of the female, the passive though fruitful element in creation, the crescent moon, the earth, darkness, water, and its emblem, a triangle with the apex downward, "the yoni"—the shallow vessel or cup for pouring fluid into (cratera), a ring or oval, a lozenge, any narrow cleft, either natural or artificial, an arch or doorway, were employed. In the same category of symbols came a boat or ship, a female date palm bearing fruit, a cow with her calf by her side, a fish, fruits having many seeds, such as the pomegranate, a shell, (concha), a cavern, a garden, a fountain, a bower, a rose, a fig, and other things of suggestive form, etc.

"These two great classes of conventional symbols were often represented *in conjunction* with each other, and thus symbolized in the highest degree the great source of life, ever originating, ever renewed . . . A similar emblem is the lingam standing in the center of the yoni, the adoration of which is to this day characteristic of the leading dogma of Hindu religion. There is scarcely a temple in India which has not its lingam, and in numerous instances this symbol is the only form under which the god Siva is worshipped."

In *Ancient Sex Worship* we read, "As the male genital organs were held in early times to exemplify the actual male creative power, various natural objects were seized upon to express the theistic idea and at the same time point to those points of the human form. Hence, a similitude is recognized in a pillar, a heap of stones, a tree between two rocks, a club between two pine cones, a trident, a thyrsus tied around with two ribbons with the end pendant, a thumb and two fingers. The caduceus again the conspicuous part of the sacred Triad Ashur is symbolized by a single stone placed upright,—the stump of a tree, a block, a tower, a spire, minaret, pole, pine, poplar or pine tree."

Hargrave Jennings, the author of several

Symbolism

books on some aspects of religions of antiquity, among them one on phallicism, deals freely with the phallic principles embodied in these religions. As do many other writers, he identifies fire worship with sex worship, and the following short paragraph shows his conception of their interrelationship, as well as the significance of the upright of antiquity. In the Rosicrucians he says: "Obelisks, spires, minarets, tall towers, upright stones, (menhirs), and architectural perpendiculars of every description, and, generally speaking, all erections conspicuous for height and slimness, were representations of the Sworded or of the Pyramidal Fire. They bespoke, wherever found and in whatever age, the idea of the First Principle or the male generative emblem."

We might readily cite passages from the writings of a number of other authors but the above paragraphs suffice to set forth the general principle of this symbolism. As stated above, such interpretations have not been generally advanced to explain such objects as sacred pillar stones, obelisks, minarets, etc. It is readily seen

Sex Worship and Symbolism

how fully these views are substantiated by observations from a number of independent sources.

In a book of Travel* in India we are able from an independent source to learn of the symbolism of that country. The traveller gives a description of the caves of Elephanta, near Bombay. These are enormous caves cut in the side of a mountain, for religious purposes to which pilgrimages are made and where the usual festivities are held. The worship of generative attributes is quite apparent. The numerous sculptured female figures, as remarked by the traveller, are all represented with greatly exaggerated breasts, a symbolism which is frequent throughout oriental countries for expressing reproductive attributes.

In an inner chamber is placed the symbol which is held in particular veneration. Here is found an upright conical stone standing within a circular one. The stone is sprinkled with water during the festival season. The writer states that this stone, to the worshippers, represents the male generative organ, and the worship of it is not considered an impropriety. In this

* Rousselet, India and Its Native Princes.

Symbolism

instance we feel that the symbolism is very definite, and doubtless the stone pillars in the other temples of India and elsewhere are of the same significance.

A clergyman in the Chinese Review of 1876, under the title *Phallic Worship in China,* gives an account of the phallicism as he observed it at that time. He states that the male sexual organ is symbolized by a simple mound of earth and is so worshipped. Similarly, the female organ is represented by a mound of different form and is worshipped as the former. The writer states that at times these mounds are built in conjunction. He states this worship is similar to that of Baal of Chaldea, etc., and that probably all have a common origin. It appears to be a fundamental part of the Chinese religion and the symbolism of the Chinese pagoda expresses the same idea. He says that Kheen or Shang-te, the Chinese deities of sex, are also worshipped in the form of serpents, of which the dragon of the Chinese is a modification. This furnishes a concrete instance in which the mound of earth is of phallic significance, and substantiates an interpretation of serpent worship to which we shall presently refer.

Hodder M. Westropp has given us an excellent account of phallic worship and includes in his description the observations of a traveller in Japan at as late periods as 1864 and 1869.

A temple near the ancient capital of Japan was visited by a traveller. In this temple the main object of worship was a large upright, standing alone, and the resemblance to the male generative organ was so striking as to leave no doubt as to what is represented. This upright was worshipped especially by women, who left votive offerings, among them small phalli, elaborately wrought out of wood or other material. The traveller remarked that the worship was most earnest and sincere.

The same traveller observed that in some of the public roads of Japan are small hedged recesses where similar pillars are found. These large pillars unquestionably represent the male organ. The writer has observed priests in procession carrying similar huge phalli, painted in color as well. This procession called forth no

PLATE V
INDIAN TEMPLE

PLATE I.
INDIAN TEMPLE.

Symbolism

particular comment and so was probably not unusual. It is stated that this is a part of the ancient "Shinto" religion of Japan and China.

There are frequent references to certain of the gods of the Ancients being represented in priapic attitudes, the phallus being the prominent and most important attribute. Thus Hermes, in Greece, was placed at cross-roads, with phallus prominent. This was comparable to the phallus on Japanese highways. In the festivals of Bacchus high phalli were carried, the male organ being represented about the size of the rest of the body. The Egyptians carried a gilt phallus, 150 cubits high, at the festivals of Osiris. In Syria, at the entrance of the temple at Hieropolis, was placed a human figure with a phallus 120 cubits high. A man mounted this upright twice a year and remained seven days, offering prayers, etc.

In Peru in the Temple of the Sun an upright pillar has been described covered with gold leaf, very similar to those existing elsewhere and to which has been ascribed similar significance.

A number of writers have expressed the belief

Sex Worship and Symbolism

that the May-pole is an emblem of ancient phallic worship. We know that May-day festivals are of the most remote antiquity. We are indebted to R. P. Knight for a description of what May-day was like about four centuries ago in England. The festival started the evening before. Men and women went out into the woods in search of a tree and brought it back to the village in the early morning. The night was spent in sexual excesses comparable to those of the Roman Bacchanalia. A procession was formed, garlands were added to the May-pole, which was set up in the village square. The Puritans referred to it as an idol, and they did not approve of the festivities. Until comparatively recent years there was a May-pole in one of the squares of London, and Samuel Pepys,* writing of his time, speaks of seeing May-poles in the front yards of the prominent citizens of Holland. A festival much the same as this was held in Ancient Rome and also in India. The May-pole properly pierces a disc and thus conforms with the lingam-yoni of India. We also know that the first of May

* Pepys Diary.

Symbolism

was a favorite time for all nature worship with the ancients. For a number of interesting suggestions the reader is referred to R. P. Knight, *Worship of Priapus* and Hargrave Jennings, *Indian Religions* (Page 66).

Tree worship is frequently mentioned in the religions of antiquity. We are told that the mystic power of the mistletoe comes from the fact that it grows on the oak, a once sacred tree. The pine of the North, the palm and the fig tree of the South, were sacred trees at one time. John Newton made a study of tree worship, especially the Ancient Grove Worship of Assyria. He shows that the object of veneration was a male date palm, which represented the Assyrian god Baal. Sex was worshipped under this deity, and it is shown that the tree of the Assyrian grove was a phallic symbol. Palm Sunday appears to be a relic of this worship. In France, until comparatively recent times, there was a festival, "La Fete des Pinnes," in which palms were carried in procession, and with the palms were carried phalli of bread which had been blessed by the priests.

Sex Worship and Symbolism

Richard Payne Knight tells us that Pan was worshipped by the Shepherds under the form of the tall fir, and Bacchus "by sticking up the rude trunk of a tree." It is shown throughout these pages that sexual attributes were worshipped under both these deities. In reference to other symbols, the writer continues;* "The spires and pinnacles with which our churches are decorated come from these ancient symbols; and the weather cocks, with which they are surmounted, though now only employed to show the direction of the wind, were originally emblems of the sun; for the cock is the natural herald of the day, and therefore sacred to the fountain of light. In the symbolical writings of the Chinese the sun is still represented by a cock in the circle; and a modern Parsee would suffer death rather than be guilty of the crime of killing one. It appears on many ancient coins, with some symbol of the passive productive power on the reverse; and in other instances it is united with priapic and other emblems and devices, signifying other attributes combined."

* Symbolic Language of Ancient Art and Mythology.

Symbolism

Dr. Thomas Inman has made a study to show this phallic symbolism found its way into ancient art, and even into some designs of modern times. Thus, many formal designs are studied in which the upright plays a part; likewise, the oval and the circle receive a similar explanation. The architectural ornaments spoken of as eggs and anchors, eggs and spear heads, the so-called honeysuckle ornament of antiquity, and the origin of some church windows and ornaments, are all studied by this writer, and his text is accompanied by illustrations. Hargrave Jennings has also traced the origin of the symbols of Heraldry, the emblems of Royalty and of some church orders with similar explanations.

We may add that the crux ansata of the Egyptians, the oval standing upon the upright, or letter Tau, may be shown to be a sex symbol, the union of the oval with the upright being of symbolic significance. The crux ansata is found in the hand of most of the Egyptian deities. It is found in the Assyrian temples and throughout the temples of India as well. Prehistoric monuments of Ireland have the same design.

Sex Worship and Symbolism

Priests are portrayed in adoration of the crux ansata before phallic monuments. The symbol, from which our modern cross is doubtless derived, originated with the religions of antiquity. Much additional evidence could readily be given to illustrate this prehistoric origin. The present Christian symbol affords another example of the adoption by a new religion of the symbols of the old.

Some reflection will show that the origin of many church customs and symbols, and indeed of a great number of obscure customs and usages, may quite properly be traced to the religions and practices of primitive races. Lafcadio Hearn has insisted upon this in the interpretation of the art and customs of the Japanese. He says,* "Art in Japan is so intimately associated with religion that any attempt to study it without extensive knowledge of the beliefs which it reflects were mere waste of time. By art I do not mean painting and sculpture but every kind of decoration, and most kinds of pictorial representation—the image of a boy's kite or a girl's

* Japan, an attempt at Interpretation.

Symbolism

battledore not less than the design upon a lacquered casquet or enameled vase,—the figure upon a workman's trowel not less than the pattern of the girdle of a princess,—the shape of the paper doll or wooden rattle bought for a baby, not less than the forms of those colossal Ni-O, who guard the gateways of the Buddha's temples," etc.

In the above pages, we have given an account of the views of a number of writers upon certain forms and symbols, and at the same time we have offered considerable evidence in substantiation from independent sources. These origins, found associated especially in art and religious usages, have not been generally understood. Yet when we reflect upon the fact that many religious customs are of great antiquity; that when once a certain form or custom becomes established, it is well nigh ineffaceable, although subject to great change or disguise throughout the centuries; when we reflect upon these conditions, and realize the fact that sex worship with its accompanying symbolism is found throughout primitive religions, we may then more readily appreciate the entire significance of the above interpretations.

It must, of course, be borne in mind that no one now gives these interpretations to spires, minarets, and to the various monumental symbols of which we have been speaking. We are here dealing exclusively with pre-historic origins, not with present day meanings. The antiquity of certain symbols is truly remarkable. The star and crescent, for example, a well known conventionalized symbol, is found on Assyrian cylinders, doubtless devised many centuries before Christ.

The full force and meaning of these various symbols may be very readily grasped by reference to a number of designs, ancient coins, bas-reliefs, monuments, etc., which have been reproduced in plates and drawings by C. W. King, Thomas Inman, R. P. Knight and others. To these we refer the reader.

A number of *plant and flower symbols* have a different significance from that which is gener-

Symbolism

ally given to them. We are all quite familiar with the grape vine of Bacchus and the association of that deity with grapes. According to R. P. Knight, this too, symbolizes a sexual attribute. Speaking of Bacchus, he writes, "The vine was a favorite symbol of the deity, which seems to have been generally employed to signify the generative or preserving attribute; intoxicating liquors were stimulative, and therefore held to be aphrodisiac. The vase is often employed in its stead to express the same idea and is often accompanied by the same accessory symbol."

We have often seen in sculptures and paintings, heads of barley associated with the God of the Harvest. This symbol would appear to be self explanatory; yet we are told by more than one writer that it contains another symbolic meaning as well. H. M. Westropp, speaking of this says, "The kites or female organ, as the symbol of the passive or productive power of nature, generally occurs on ancient Roman Monuments as the Concha Veneris, a fig, barley corn, and the letter Delta." We are told that the grain of barley, because of its form, was a symbol of the vulva.

A great many other female symbols might be mentioned. The pomegranate is constantly seen in the hands of Proserpine. The fir-cone is carried by the Assyrian Baal, and the fig in numerous processions has a similar significance. When we add to these the various forms of tree worship described above, we see to what an extent the products of nature were used as symbols in the worship of sex.

Among flower symbols there is one which recurs constantly throughout the art and mythology of India, Egypt, China, and many other Eastern countries. This is the lotus, of which the Easter lily is the modern representative. The lotus appears in a number of forms in the records of antiquity. We have symbolic pictures of the lion carrying the lotus in its mouth, doubtless a male and female symbol. The deities of India are depicted standing on the lotus, or are spoken of as being "born of the Lotus." "The Chinese,"* says the author of Rites and Ceremonies, "worship a Goddess whom they call

* O'Brien: The Round Towers of Ireland.

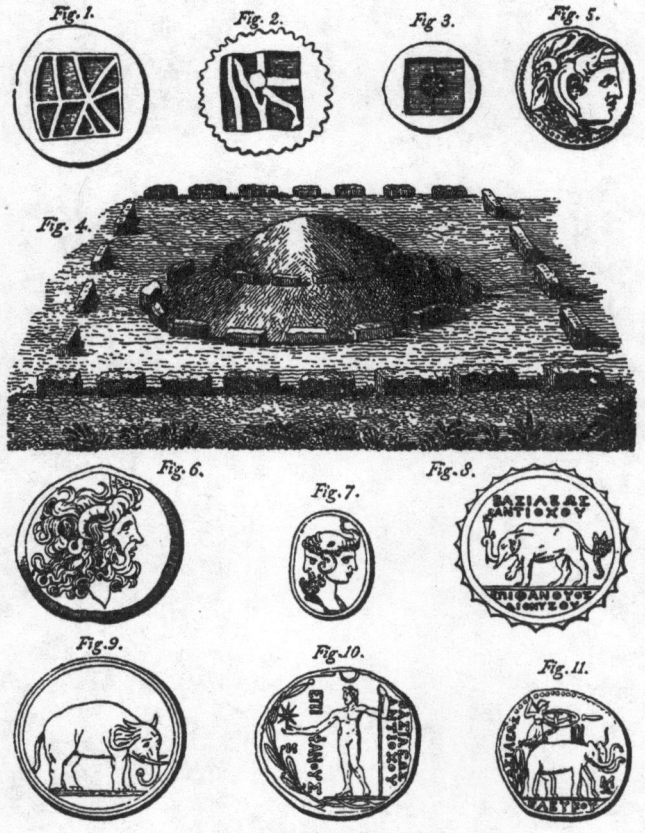

PLATE VI
CELTIC TEMPLE AND GREEK MEDALS

Fig. 1 Talisman square on Greek medal. 2 Egyptian talisman. 3 Asterisk of the sun in center of square on Syracuse medal. 4 Celtic Temple in Zeeland. 5 Minerva with an elephant's skin on her head. 6 Horns as symbol of power. 7 Minerva represented in the Indian manner with the elephant skin over her helmet. 8 Deity represented by an elephant bearing the torch (male symbol) in his trunk and the cornucopia (female symbol) in his tail. 9 Horns of the bull placed on the head of the elephant. 10 Jupiter with the moon on his head and the sun in his hand. 11 Minerva holding spear.

Symbolism

Puzza, and of whom their priests give the following acount;—they say that 'three nymphs came down from heaven to wash themselves in the river, but scarce had they gotten in the water before the herb lotus appeared on one of their garments, with its coral fruit upon it. They were surprised to think whence it could proceed; and the nymph upon whose garment it was could not resist the temptation of indulging herself in tasting it. But by thus eating some of it she became pregnant, and was delivered of a boy, whom she brought up, and then returned to heaven. He afterwards became a great man, a conqueror and legislator, and the nymph was afterwards worshipped under the name of Puzza.'" Puzza corresponds to the Indian Buddha.

In Egyptian architecture the lotus is a fundamental form, and indeed it is said to be the main motive of the architecture of that civilization. The capitals of the column are modelled after one form or other of this plant. That of the Doric column is the seed vessel pressed flat. Earlier capitals are simple copies of the bell or seed vessel. The columns consisted of stalks of the plant grouped together. In other cases the leaves are used as ornaments. These orders were copied by the Greeks, and subsequently by western countries.

We may ask ourselves, what is the meaning of this mystic lotus which was held in sufficient veneration to be incorporated in all the temples of religions, as well as in myths of the deity. This, too, refers to the deification of sex. O'Brien, in the *Round Towers of Ireland* states: "The lotus was the most sacred plant of the Ancients, and typified the two principles of the earth fecundation,—the germ standing for the lingam; the filaments and petals for the yoni."

R. P. Knight states, "We find it (the lotus) employed in every part of the Northern Hemisphere where symbolical worship does or ever did prevail. The sacred images of the Tartars, Japanese or Indians, are all placed upon it and it is still sacred in Tibet and China. The upper part of the base of the lingam also consists of the flower of it blended with the most distinctive characteristics of the female sex; in which that

Symbolism

of the male is placed, in order to complete this mystic symbol of the ancient religion of the Brahmans; who, in their sacred writings, speak of Brahma sitting upon his lotus throne."

Alexander Wilder,* states that the term "Nymphe" and its derivations were used to designate young women, brides, the marriage chamber, the lotus flower, oracular temples and the labiae minores of the human female.

The lotus then, which is found throughout antiquity, in art as well as in religion, was a sexual symbol, representing to the ancients the combination of male and female sexual organs. It is another expression of the sex worship of that period.

Our present conventional symbols of art are very easily traced to ancient symbols of religion. We may expect these to be phallic in their meaning, to just the extent that phallicism was fundamental in the religions where these symbols originated. From the designs of some of the ornamental friezes of Nineveh, we find these principles illustrated. On those bas-reliefs is

* The Symbolical Language of Ancient Art and Mythology.

found the earliest form of art, really the dawn of art upon early civilization. Here is the beginning of certain designs which were destined to be carried to the later civilizations of Greece, Rome and probably of Egypt. These friezes show the pine cone alternating with a modified form of the lotus; the significance of which symbols we have explained. There are also shown animal representations before the sacred tree or grove, a phallic symbol. From these forms and others were designed a number of conventional symbols which were used throughout a much later civilization. (See *Nineveh and Its Remains*. A. Layard.)

One sees in the religions of antiquity, especially those of India, Assyria, Greece and Egypt, a great number of *sacred animal representations*. The Bull was sacred to Osiris in Egypt, and one special animal was attended with all the pomp of a god. At one time in Assyria the god was always associated with a sacred animal, often the goat, which was supposed to possess the qualities for which the god was worshipped.

Symbolism

Out of this developed the ideal animal creations, of which the animal body and the human head and the winged bulls of Nineveh are examples. The mystic centaurs and satyrs originated from this source. At a later time the whole was humanized, merely the horns, ears or hoofs remaining as relics of the animal form.

We learn that in these religions the animal was not merely worshipped as such. It was a certain quality which was deified. The Assyrian goat attendant upon the deity, was in some bas-reliefs, not only represented in priapic attitudes, but a female sexual symbol was so placed as to signify sexual union. We shall show later that certain male and female symbolic animals were so placed on coins as to symbolically indicate sexual union.

An animal symbol which has probably been of universal use is that of the snake or serpent. Serpent worship has been described in almost every country of which we have records or legends. In Egypt, we find the serpent on the headdress of many of the gods. In Africa the snake is still sacred with many tribes. The

Sex Worship and Symbolism

worship of the hooded snake was probably carried from India to Egypt. The dragon on the flag and porcelain of China is also a serpent symbol. In Central America were found enormous stone serpents carved in various forms. In Scandinavia divine honors were paid to serpents, and the druids of Britain carried on a similar worship.

Serpent worship has been shown by many writers to be a form of sex worship. It is often phallic, and we are told by Hargrave Jennings that the serpent possibly was added to the male and female symbols to represent desire. Thus, the Hindu women carried the lingam in procession between two serpents; and in the procession of Bacchus the Greeks carried in a casket the phallus, the egg, and a serpent.

The Greeks also had a composite or ideal figure. Rays were added to the head of a serpent thereby bringing it into relation with the sun god Apollo; or the crest or comb of a cock was added with similar meaning.

Many reasons have been offered to explain why the serpent has been used to represent the male

Symbolism

generative attribute. Some have called attention to its tenacity of life; others have spoken of its supposed mystic power of regeneration by casting its skin. Again, it seems probable that the form is of symbolic significance. However this may be, we find that this universal serpent worship of primitive man was a form of phallicism so prevalent in former times.

Many other animals may be mentioned. The sacred bull, so frequently met with in Egypt, Assyria and Greece, was a form under which Bacchus was worshipped. R. P. Knight speaks as follows: "The mystic Bacchus, or generative power, was represented under this form, not only upon coins but upon the temples of the Greeks; sometimes simply as a bull; at other times as a human face; and at others entirely human except the horns and ears."

We would probably be in error to interpret all these animal symbols as exclusively phallic although many were definitely so. Thus, while Hermes was a priapic deity, he was also a deity of the fields and the harvests; so the bull may have been chosen for its strength as well as its sexual attributes.

There are many animals which were symbolic of the female generative power. The cow is frequently so employed. The Hindus have the image of a cow in nearly every temple, the deity corresponding to the Grecian Venus. In the temple of Philae in Egypt, Isis is represented with the horns and ears of a cow joined to a beautiful woman. The cow is still sacred in many parts of Africa. The fish symbol was a very frequent representative of woman, the goddess of the Phoenicians being represented by the head and body of a woman terminating below in a fish. The head of Proserpine is frequently surrounded by dolphins. Indeed, the female principle is regularly shown by some representative of water; fire and water respectively being regarded as male and female principles.

Male and female attributes are often combined on coins for purposes of sexual symbolism. R. P. Knight explains these symbols as follows: "It appears therefore that the asterisk, bull, or minotaur, in the centre of a square or labyrinth

Symbolism

equally mean the same as the Indian lingam,— that is the male personification of the productive attribute blaced in the female, or heat acting upon humidity. Sometimes the bull is placed between two dolphins, and sometimes upon a dolphin or another fish; and in other instances the goat or the ram occupy the same position. Which are all different modes of expressing different modifications of the same meaning in symbolical or mystical writings. The female personifications frequently occupy the same place; in which case the male personification is always upon the reverse of the coin, of which numerous instances occur in those of Syracuse, Naples, Tarentum, and other cities." By the asterisk above mentioned the writer refers to a circle surrounded by rays, a sun symbol of male significance. The square or labyrinth is the lozenge shaped symbol or yoni of India.

The above interpretations throw much light on the obscurity of the animal worship of antiquity. This explains the partly humanized types, and the final appearance of a human deity with only animal horns remaining, as representing the form under which the deity was once worshipped. The satyrs, centaurs, and other animal forms are all part of these same representations and are similarly explained.

Our main object in giving the above account of these various symbols has been to illustrate the wide prevalence of sex worship among primitive races. Another end as well has been served; our study gives us a certain insight into the type of mind which evolves symbolism, and so a few remarks on the use of symbolism as here illustrated are not inappropriate.

We feel that while this symbolism may indicate a high degree of mechanical skill in execution, it does not follow that it expresses either deep or complicated intellectual processes. In fact, we are inclined to regard such symbolism as the indication of a comparatively simple intellect. It appears obscure and involved to us, because we do not understand the symbols. From those which we do understand, the meaning is graphically but simply expressed.

On coins, bas-reliefs and monuments, we find

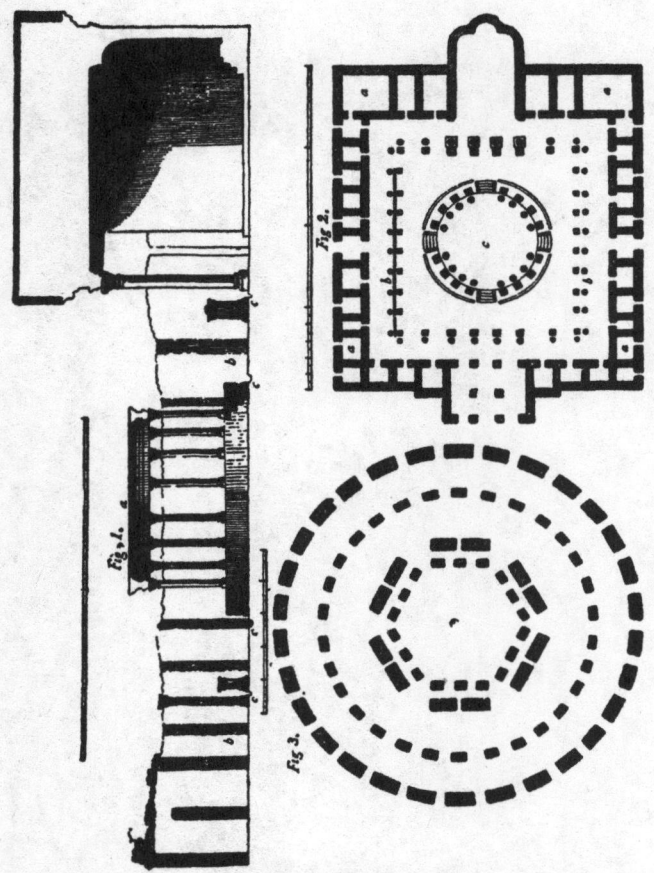

PLATE VII
TEMPLE DEDICATED TO BACCHUS AT PUZZUOLI

Fig. 1 (a) Holy of Holies.
      (b) Showing distance below level of the ground.
      (c) Drains and conduits for flooding temple.
Fig. 2 (a) Apartments of priests.
      (b) Portico.
      (c) Holy of Holies.
Fig. 3 Circular of temple.

Symbolism

the majority of these simple emblems. If the desire is to express the union of male and female principles, a male symbolic animal is simply placed upon the corresponding female symbol. Thus, a goat or bull may be placed upon the back of a dolphin or other fish. This is a graphic presentation but certainly one of a most simple nature. Sometimes the male symbol is on one side of the coin and then the female is always on the reverse. Unions are made which do not occur in nature, and the representation is not a subtle one.

In India, if there was a desire to express a number of attributes of the deity, another head or face is added or additional arms are added to hold up additional symbols. In Greece, when the desire was to express the androgyne qualities of the deity, a beard was added to the female face, or one-half of the statuette represented the male form, the other the female. Such representations do not indicate great ingenuity, however skillfully they may be executed.

SUN MYTHS, MYSTERIES AND DECADENT SEX WORSHIP

CHAPTER III

SUN MYTHS, MYSTERIES AND DECADENT SEX WORSHIP

AS is generally known, traces of sun worship are found in almost every country of which we have a record. In Egypt Ra was the supreme sun god where there was very elaborate worship conducted in his honor. In Greece, Apollo was attended with similar festivities. In the Norse mythology, many of the myths deal with the worship of the sun in one form or another. In England, Stonehenge and the entire system of the Druids had to do with solar worship. In Central America and Peru, temples to the sun were of amazing splendor, furnished as they were with wonderful displays of gold and silver. The North American Indians have many legends relating to sun worship and sacrifices to the sun, and China and Japan give numerous instances of the same religion. Sun worship is so readily shown to be fundamental with primitive races that we will not discuss it in detail at this time, but rather will give the conclusions of certain writers who have explained its meaning.

At the present day, the sun is regularly regarded as a male being, the earth a female. We speak of Mother Earth, etc.; in former times, the ancients depicted the maternal characteristics of the earth in a much more material way. Likewise the sun was a male deity, being often the war god, vigorous and all powerful. We readily see to what an extent the male sun god was portrayed in mythology as a human being. In many myths, the god dies during the Winter, reappears in the Spring, is lamented in the Fall, etc., all in keeping with the changes in the activity of the sun during the different seasons.

The moon was associated with the female deity of the ancients. Isis is accompanied by the moon on most coins and emblems. Venus has the same symbols. Indeed, the star and crescent of our modern times, of the Turkish flag and elsewhere, are in reality the sun and crescent of antiquity,

Mysteries and Decadent Worship

male and female symbols in conjunction. Lunar ornaments of prehistoric times have been found throughout England and Ireland, and doubtless explain the superstitions about the moon in those countries. The same prehistoric ornaments are found in Italy. In legends of the North American Indians, Moon is Sun's wife.

The full extent of these beliefs is pointed out by Mr. John Newton in *Assyrian Grove Worship*. Here we see that the ancient Hindus gave a much more literal relationship between the sun and earth than we are accustomed to express in modern times. He states, "This representative of the union of the sexes typifies the divine Sakti, or productive energy, in union with the procreative or generative power as seen throughout nature. The earth was the primitive pudendum or yoni which is fecundated by the solar heat, the sun, the primitive linga, to whose vivifying rays man and animals, plants and the fruits of the earth, owe their being and continued existence."

It is not possible to discuss sun worship at any length without at the same time discussing phallicism and serpent worship. Hargrave Jennings, who has made careful study of these worships, points out their general identity in the following paragraph. He states: "The three most celebrated emblems carried in the Greek mysteries were the phallus, the egg, and the serpent; or otherwise the phallus, the yoni or umbilicus, and the serpent. The first in each case is the emblem of the sun or of fire, as the male or active generative power. The second denotes the passive nature or female principle or the emblem of water. The third symbol indicates the destroyer, the reformer or the renewer, (the uniter of the two) and thus the preserver or perpetuator eternally renewing itself. The universality of serpentine worship (or Phallic adoration) is attested by emblematic sculptures or architecture all the world over."

The author of the *Round Towers of Ireland* in discussing the symbols of sun worship, serpent worship and phallicism, found on the same tablet, practically reiterates these statements. He says: "I have before me the sameness of design which belonged indifferently to solar

Mysteries and Decadent Worship

worship and to phallic. I shall, ere long, prove that the same characteristic extends equally to ophiolatreia; and if they all three be identical, as it thus necessarily follows, where is the occasion for surprise at our meeting the sun, phallus and serpent, the constituent symbols of each, embossed upon the same table and grouped under the same architrave?"

By a number of references, we could readily show the identity of all these worships. The preceding paragraphs give, in summary form, the conclusions of those writers who have made such religions their special study. We shall not exemplify this further, but will now point out the general relationship of sun worship to the religious festivals and mythology of the Ancients. This relationship becomes important when it is appreciated that the sun worship expressed in the mysteries is also a part of phallicism. On some of these festive occasions the phallus was carried in the front of the procession and at other times the egg, the phallus and the serpent were carried in the secret casket.

Sex Worship and Symbolism

The Ancients expressed their religious beliefs in a dramatic way on a number of occasions throughout the year. The festivities were held in the Spring, Autumn, or Winter. These were to commemorate the activities of the sun, his renewed activity in the Spring calling forth rejoicing and his decline in the Fall being the cause of sorrow and lamentation. As well as the festivities, there were the various mysteries, such as the Eleusinia, the Dionysia and the Bacchanalia. These were conducted by the priests who moulded religious beliefs and guarded their secrets. The mysteries were of the utmost importance and the most sacred of religious conceptions were here dramatized.

Mythology also gave expression to the religious ideas of the time and we find that the most important myths, dramatically produced at the religious festivals, were sun myths.

The annual festivities and mysteries will be discussed together because both were intended to dramatize the same beliefs. Both were under priestly control and so were national institutions. The festivals were for the common people but the

PLATE VIII
ORNNAMENT FROM PUZZUOLI TEMPLE

Fig. 1 Wolf devouring grapes as destructive power of sun.
Fig. 2 Deity crowned with laurel wreath.

Mysteries and Decadent Worship

mysteries were fully understood only to the initiated.

While no very clear account of the mysteries has been given, a certain theme seems to run through them all, and this is found in the myths as well. A drama is enacted, in which the god is lost, is lamented, and is found or returns amid great rejoicing.* This was enacted in Egypt where the mourning was for Osiris; and in Greece for Adonis, and later for Bacchus. All these are, of course, sun gods, and the whole dramatization or myth is in keeping with the activities of the sun.

On these occasions, the main object seems to have been to restore the lost god, or to insure his reappearance. The women took the leading part and mourned for Osiris, Adonis or Bacchus. They wandered about the country at night in the most frenzied fashion, avoided all men and sought the god. At times, during the winter festival, the quest would be fruitless. In the Spring, when they indulged themselves in all

* The Enactment of a Rebirth.

sorts of orgies and extravagances, Adonis was found.

An underlying motive appears to have been to enact a drama in which the deity was supposed to exercise his procreative function by sexual union with the women. This was an ideal which they wished to express dramatically. In order to realize this ideal obstacles were introduced that they might be overcome; in the old myth, Adonis was emasculated under a pine tree, and in Egypt Osiris was similarly mutilated, his sex organs being lost. But at the festivals it was portrayed that Adonis was found, and in the myth, Osiris was restored to Isis in the form of Horus (the morning sun). In a number of myths the god is said to have visited the earth to cohabitate with the women, an occurrence which was doubtless desired, in order that the deistic attributes might be continued in the race. Thus, judging from what we have been able to learn of this subject, the worship expressed in the mysteries revolved about sexual union, the desire being to dramatize the continued activity of deistic qualities.

Mysteries and Decadent Worship

This character of many of the festivals and mysteries is very evident. In the Eleusinian mysteries the rape of Persephone by Pluto, the winter god, is portrayed. The mother, Demeter, mourns for her daughter. Her mourning is dramatically carried out by a large procession, and this enactment requires several days. Finally Persephone is restored. The earlier part of the festival was for dramatic interest, and the real object was the union of Persephone with Bacchus. "The union of Persephone with Bacchus, *i. e.*, with the sun god, whose work is to promote fruitfulness, is an idea special to the mysteries and means the union of humanity with the godhead, the consummation aimed at in the mystic rites. Hence, in all probability the central teaching of the mysteries was Personal Immortality, analogue of the return of the bloom to plants in Spring."*

The mysteries of Samothrace were probably simpler. Here the phallus was carried in procession as the emblem of Hermes. In the Dionysian mysteries which were held in mid-

* Dr. Otto Rhyn, Mysteria.

winter, the quest of the women was unsuccessful and the festival was repeated in the Spring. The Roman mysteries of Bacchus were of much later development, and consequently became very debased. Men as well as women eventually came to take part in the ceremony, and the whole affair degenerated into the grossest of sexual excesses and perversions.

We have stated what appears to us to have been the underlying motives of the religious festivals and mysteries; namely, the enactment of a drama in which the reproductive qualities of the deity were portrayed. The phallus was carried in procession for this purpose and the women dramatized the motive as searching for the god. Our account can be regarded as little more than an outline, but it is sufficient for our present purposes. It indicates that the mysteries give an impression of phallic worship, just as do the various monuments of art and religion to which we have referred. It may also be said that this same worship is represented in what may be termed early literature, for much of the early mythology deals with the same subject. The

Mysteries and Decadent Worship

study of origins in mythology, however, cannot be dealt with adequately at present.

In order to deal fully with this subject it is necessary to discuss another important phase in the worship of sex. We refer to the *decadence or degeneracy of this worship,* which occurred after people had outgrown these simple religious conceptions. The decadence of sex worship is observed during the early centuries of Christianity and traces of it are seen throughout the middle ages. In the decadence of sex worship we are able to observe how an important motive in the race finds expression in the thoughts and conduct of people after the underlying promptings which originated it have long since ceased to be dynamic. This decadent stage of a motive is therefore of considerable importance; we shall return to its interpretation in the discussion of analogies of development between motives in the individual and motives in the race.

In India,[*] with the Hindus, there still exists an elaborate form of sex worship. The Phallus

[*] J. B. Pratt, India and Its Faiths.

Sex Worship and Symbolism

is carried on festive occasions, it still occupies the most sacred spot in the sanctuary, dancing girls are devoted to the service of the temple, and many other customs associated with phallic rites are carried on much as they were centuries ago in the Ancient World. It is said that there are thirty million phalli in India and that a phallus is found in nearly every Hindu household.

Whether phallic worship as now practiced by the Hindus has the same meaning or value that it had when at its height in ancient civilization is difficult to say; there are evidences to show that this worship in India is now carried out somewhat as a matter of form and custom only, and that its significance is not thoroughly appreciated except possibly by the few. If this observation is correct, the decadent state of sex worship which was so prevalent in Western Europe during the early centuries of Christianity and throughout the middle ages, may be developing in India as well.

Whatever may be the present condition in India regarding this worship, we are left in no

Mysteries and Decadent Worship

uncertainty as to the condition of sex worship during its decadent period in Europe. It is not necessary here to dwell upon the licentiousness and extravagances of conduct which were manifest at this time, as a general outline will suffice for present purposes.

We have observed that the mysteries in which phallic principles were taught eventually became degraded in both Greece and Rome. When these mysteries originated, they embodied serious religious conceptions, respected by all; they were the expression of racial feelings, and however out of accord with present day sentiments they may have been, they can in no way be considered immoral. This cannot be said of the mysteries of a subsequent period. Every sort of perversion and practice was indulged in. They were finally forbidden by the State, but were carried on secretly for some time longer. With the coming of Christianity they were very bitterly opposed, and finally as national institutions, they ceased to exist.

Later we shall indicate in more detail why the worship of sex was discarded. It may be stated here that as the development of the race continued these simple conceptions of a deity failed to express all religious desires; primitive phallic principles lost their dynamic value, and longings and desires, the result of higher mental development, found expression in new religious usages.

It has just been stated that the mysteries ceased to exist as national institutions. This is true, but while they were discarded by the great mass of the people, certain elements of the race clung to these primitive beliefs and practices for years. When the mysteries were officially forbidden they were carried on secretly in a somewhat altered form. Secret societies were formed, or some of the Eastern Mystic Cults were made use of in order to carry out their teachings. These secret societies took over many of the principles of phallicism such as were taught in the mysteries, and so, side by side with the Christian religion, the earlier beliefs continued.

The Gnostics* are an example of one of these societies. They existed in early Christian times and the society was probably formed long before

* R. P. Knight, the Worship of Priapus.

Mysteries and Decadent Worship

the advent of Christianity. It is difficult to learn a great deal about the Gnostics, but some of their beliefs are known. Gnostic symbols consisted for a great part of phallic emblems, it having been shown that their gems and secret talismans were of phallic significance. The Gnostics also gave evidences of reverting to a more primitive civilization in other than religious spheres. In their social organization they advocated communal marriage, wives being held in common. This type of social organization is quite general in primitive tribes. With the Gnostics we see a reversion to a more primitive form of religious and social life.

The Rosicrucians* of the middle ages are rather better known, although this order also is very obscure. The Rosicrucians as well as the Gnostics had phallic emblems. They worshipped in a form very similar to that under which Priapus was worshipped. Moreover, as was the case with a number of these secret societies, they

* Hargrave Jennings: The Rosicrucians.

introduced perverse sexual practices. They are said not only to have countenanced homosexuality, but to have made it one of the principles of their belief. At the same time, they scorned all association with women. Out of this belief they built up a philosophy in which the fire worship of antiquity played a part, and with which alchemy was associated.

In the practice of homosexuality* and in the development of a philosophy in which women played no part, are seen sentiments quite similar to those which existed in the later days of Greece. At this time in Greece, patriarchy had driven out the last vestiges of matriarchy, female deities had lost their followers to a great extent, and the devotion was paid to male gods and heroes. This change seems to have produced a certain contempt for women. A number of writers have pointed out this reaction, and so probably in the philosophy of the Rosicrucians and in their practices, are seen an expression of these same

* J. A. Symonds, A Problem in Greek Ethics. Morris J. Karpas, Socrates in the Light of Modern Psychopathology. Journal of Abnormal Psychology. 1915.

PLATE IX
ORNAMENT FROM PUZZUOLI TEMPLE

Mysteries and Decadent Worship

sentiments. Similar sentiments were expressed by other secret organizations and in some philosophies of a latter period. In this respect, therefore, the Rosicrucians were probably reverting to beliefs and feelings of an earlier date.

The Knights Templar were another secret society of the middle ages of a somewhat later time. The same can be said of them as of the former societies. They carried on the old phallic and mystic rites in modified form, and set up their beliefs in opposition to Christianity. When the Knights Templar were initiated they were made to deny Christ and the Virgin Mary, to spit on the cross, etc. They also were charged with homosexuality, and with them as with the Rosicrucians and the Gnostics, homosexuality was a part of their teachings. They likewise advocated communal marriage. At their secret meetings and initiations many vices existed; idols were worshipped, phallic features were introduced, and the entire ceremony was similar to the mysteries of antiquity.

Should there be any doubt regarding the association of these secret societies of the middle ages with the mysteries of the Ancients, this doubt is at once dispelled when we read of the practices of a remarkable secret organization described as the "Witches' Sabbath." Any one who has read a description of the Ancient Mysteries and of the initiation ceremonies of primitive tribes cannot but see in the Witches' Sabbath a remarkable similarity to the earlier mysteries. R. P. Knight* has given us a description of the Witches' Sabbath and he quotes freely from a French writer† who has given full details. We shall use such parts of these descriptions as are necessary to illustrate these practices during the middle ages.

The Witches' Sabbath is described by these writers as it existed during the latter part of the fourteenth century. It was held on four occasions during the year, being a festival corresponding to the Priapiea and Bacchanalia of former days. Women played the leading part just as in the Bacchanalia. There were minor and major festivals corresponding to the lesser

* Worship of Priapus.
† Pierre de Lancre, Tableau de l'Inconstance des Mauvais Anges et Démons.

Mysteries and Decadent Worship

and greater Eleusinia. Pilgrimages were made at this time, which "resembled a fair of merchants mingled together, furious in transports, arriving from all parts—a meeting and a mingling of a hundred thousand subjects, sudden and transitory, novel, it is true, but of a frightful novelty which offends the eye and sickens you."

A symbolic representation of Satan presided at the festivals, and he assumed a number of disguises, in all of which we recognize Priapus in degenerated form. He very often appeared in the disguise of a goat; in fact the meeting place is called "Goat's Heath."

The association of the goat with priapic ceremonies has already been mentioned. At times the meeting was at cross roads, a favorite location for Hermes, as stated elsewhere.

Satan assumed a number of forms on these occasions other than that of the bearded goat. He was at times a serpent, or again an ox of brass. He was also represented as the trunk of a tree, sometimes as the oak. Priapus is readily recognized in all these various disguises.

On these festive occasions we see remnants

of the fire worship of primitive tribes. Satan often carried fire in some form or other and the rite of purification by fire, a residual of the earlier need-fire rites, was enacted. Particular significance was attached to the generative organs, and it is needless to say that all kinds of sexual excesses ensued. Satan was held to be the father and protector of all. Some of the women referred to the Witches' Sabbath as an earthly paradise and they said that the festival had all the features of a wedding celebration.

A number of absurd dances and other burlesques were introduced. In these one sees the burlesques and dances of the earlier mysteries and of the still more primitive initiation ceremonies of tribes in various countries. The dance was often held around a stone,—the significance of which has already been explained.

If in the above account of these mystic ceremonies in the middle ages a detailed enumeration of all forms of sexual depravities has not been given, it is not because they did not exist. Our main object has been to show that sex worship as practiced during the middle ages, was an ex-

Mysteries and Decadent Worship

pression of the decadence of a racial motive. No odium was formerly connected with this motive, but when an attempt was made to associate these primitive feelings and beliefs with a civilization which had outgrown such conceptions, many undesirable features were in evidence.

Should further proof of the association of the Gnostics, the Rosicrucians, the Templars, etc., with the ancient priapic rites be necessary, this proof is found in numerous talismans, amulets, sculpture on earthen and glassware, which were associated with these societies. These amulets are all plainly phallic in design; R. P. Knight shows a number of vases, lamps, etc., on which phallic symbols are found. These articles were probably used at the secret rites.

Moreover, we find that many of these small phalli were worn for personal decoration; and here we come to a still lower decadence in sex worship,—the period of superstition. A phallus was worn as a charm, somewhat as a fetish to ward off disease. Such charms were supposed to bring good luck and prosperity to the owner and they were used particularly as a charm aaginst barreness in women. A sign which could be made by the hand, the phallic hand, was used as a protection against the evil eye. Ancient representations of Priapus have been found with the hand in this attitude. As further evidence to show the total degeneracy of these beliefs, it may be said that the phallic hand was adopted as a symbol of prostitution.

In this we see the worship of sex degenerated to its lowest form, *i. e.*, a superstition to be followed by the lower classes and the ignorant. The phallus which once had been attended with all ceremony had become a mere charm.

The conclusions which R. P. Knight reaches in relation to these decadent beliefs are worthy of remark. He states:* "We have thus seen in how many various forms the old phallic, or priapic worship presented itself in the middle ages, and how pertinaciously it held its ground through all the changes and development of society, until at length we find all the circumstances of the ancient priapic orgies, as well as the mediaeval additions combined in that great

* Worship of Priapus.

Mysteries and Decadent Worship

and extensive superstition,—witchcraft. At all times the initiated were believed to have obtained thereby powers which were not possessed by the uninitiated, and they only were supposed to know about the form of invocation of the deities who were the objects of this worship, which deities the Christian teachers invariably transformed into devils. The vows which people of antiquity addressed to Priapus, those of the middle ages addressed to Satan. The Witches' Sabbath was simply the last form which the Priapeia and Libernalia assumed in Western Europe, and in its various decadences all the incidents of those great and licentious orgies of the Romans were reproduced." It is little wonder that the persecution of witches by the Christians long survived the middle ages.

Hargrave Jennings* has referred to phallic principles in a number of the early chivalric societies of England. He states that the Knights of the Round Table of King Arthur had phallic emblems and other features similar to those of

* The Rosicrucians.

the Rosicrucians. The same author submits considerable evidence to indicate that the Order of the Garter is of much greater antiquity than is generally believed and that phallic principles were associated with it. A similar contention was made regarding the symbolism associated with the Holy Grail, a sacred vessel apparently connected with primitive rites at a time far antedating Christianity. Associated with the old Churches in Ireland similar phallic emblems have been found, as well as in Europe. These emblems were used as charms by the primitive people.

We stated above that the early deities of primitive tribes were regarded as demons during the Christian period. In Teutonic beliefs phallic deities were developed quite comparable to those of Greece and Rome. These Teutonic deities came to be regarded as hobgoblins during the middle ages. They were supposed to be found in lonely places and in forests, and to emerge at times in order to indulge in all sorts of sexual excesses, much as the fauns and satyrs of an-

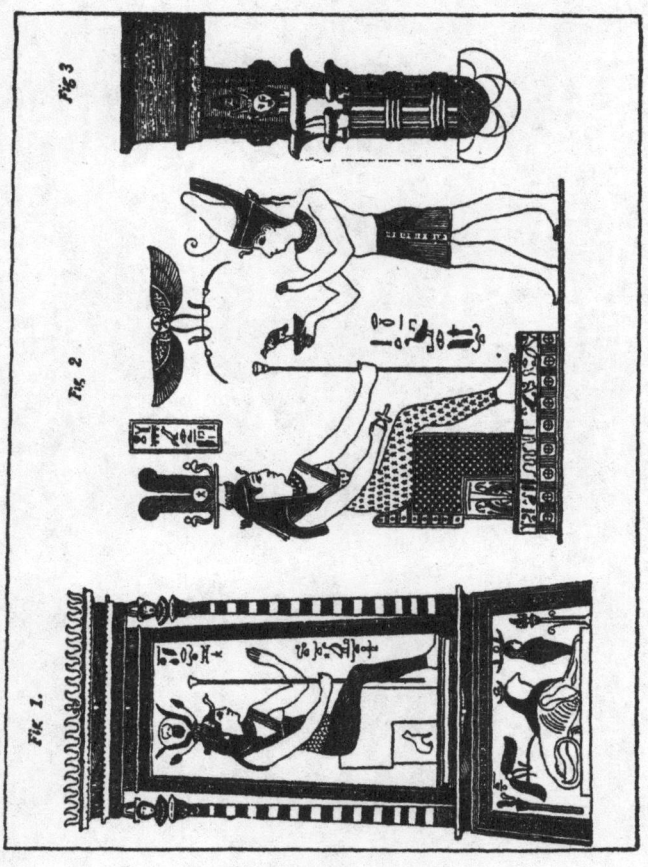

PLATE X
EGYPTIAN FIGURES AND ORNAMENTS

Fig. 1 Columns like the lotus which Isis holds.
Fig. 2 Isis holding the stem of the lotus surmounted by the seed-vessel in one hand and the cross in the other.
Fig. 3 Horns and ears of cow on head of Venus.

Mysteries and Decadent Worship

tiquity. The English had a similar hobgoblin in Robin Goodfellow. This fictitious character is represented in priapic attitudes in a number of illustrations of old English ballads. He was doubtless Priapus of antiquity transformed into a goblin.

Why should superstitions of this kind live century after century? Frazer* has given us the answer: "Superstitions survive because while they shock the views of the enlightened members of the community, they are still in harmony with the thoughts and feelings of others, who, though they are drilled by their betters into an appearance of civilization, remain barbarians or savages at heart . . . I have been led into making these remarks by the wish to explain why it is that superstitions of all sorts, political, moral and religious, survive among people who have the opportunity of knowing better. The reason is that the better ideas, which are constantly forming in the upper stratum have not filtered through from the highest to the lowest minds.

* The Scope of Social Anthropology; Psyche's Task.

Sex Worship and Symbolism

Such a filtration is generally slow, and by the time the new emotions have penetrated to the bottom, if indeed they ever get there, they are often obsolete and superseded by others at the top."

INTERPRETATIONS

CHAPTER IV

INTERPRETATIONS

HAVING followed the worship of sex through its various phases, it is now desirable to offer such interpretations of its meaning as the facts appear to warrant. What was the significance of this elaborate ritual; why did it develop, and how is it to be interpreted from a biological standpoint in mental evolution. The history of the development of this ritual may be of considerable interest in itself but we wish now to consider the subject from the biological rather than the historical standpoint. It remains to be shown what ends these beliefs serve in the evolution of the primitive mind, or at least what they represent, and what vestiges of them remain in our thoughts and feelings of today. Only from this standpoint can the study of primitive motives be of value to the Psychologist and the Psychiatrist.

Sex Worship and Symbolism

In order to answer the above questions, it is desirable to refer to a still more primitive form of religious belief, since our understanding of this earlier religion offers a key to the understanding of sex worship. We refer to the various forms of nature worship found in primitive tribes. These nature rites consist of rain making ceremonies, sun dances, and numerous other procedures which are carried out by primitive people because of their supposed service in increasing the products of the earth. Fortunately these rites are quite clearly understood. It has been shown by many investigators that they are enacted to increase the food supply. They are actuated by the desire on the part of primitive people to meet nutritive demands.

Now this knowledge enables us to understand phallic ceremonies. A very distinct parallelism is seen between the nature worship rites and phallic rites. We feel that it is not difficult to show that while the earlier rites were in accord with nutritive demands, phallic ceremonies were an expression of the desire for human reproduction. We shall now digress somewhat in order

Interpretations

to discuss nature rites in some detail, as thereby the phallic rites are very readily explained.

Among many of the Indian tribes of North America, the tribes of Central Africa, the primitive races of Australia, the lower hill tribes of India, and others, we find religious ceremonies all of which are carried out in much the same way and with the same object in view. We are all familiar with the rain making ceremonies of the North American Indians; we find frequent reference in literature to the various Spring festivals of the Egyptians at which grain is grown, etc., and in which vegetative nature is deified. A great many of the nations of antiquity had similar rites to increase the produce of the earth.

When the meaning of this general type of ceremony is understood, it is found that it has the same significance throughout. As stated above, these ceremonies are enacted to increase the food supply, either directly or indirectly. If it is a dry and arid locality, as is the case with our Western Indians, a rain making rite is performed. This is a religious procedure in which various processes of magic are utilized. This explains the importance of the thunder god as a deity, so clearly illustrated by Miss J. Harrison. The thunder rites are to increase the rain fall, and the magic in such procedures is imitative; that is, a sound similar to thunder is produced, as primitive man believes thunder to cause the rainfall since it often precedes it. Miss Harrison* has given a picture of an early thunder god of the Chinese,—a deity surrounded by many objects, which he strikes to cause thunder. Rattles made of gourds are used for the same purpose with some tribes; or down, etc., may be used in imitation of clouds, and water spurted about to represent rain. In many instances a secret ceremonial object is used,—a bull roarer in the rain making ceremonies. This is an object which, when whirled about, makes a sound in imitation of thunder. It represents a sort of thunder deity and so is associated with rainfall. It is held very sacred, being carefully guarded from view and kept under custody by the head men of the tribe.

* Themis.

Interpretations

In a primitive civilization engaged in pastoral pursuits where the herd is the important source of food supply the ceremony centers about the dairy and the herd. In Southern India, among the Toda tribes,[*] where the buffalo herd is sacred, this is quite apparent. Certain buffaloes are attended by the priests only, special dairies are sacred, and the entire religious development has to do with the sanctity of milk. The dairy utensils are sacred, and one special vessel, the one which contains the fermenting material, is held in particular veneration. This vessel is kept in a special part of the dairy, its location corresponding to the sanctuary of a temple. If by chance the ferment does not act properly, it is manufactured again by an elaborate rite. Here we see that the religious rites have to do with the food supply and fitting sacred ceremonials are performed.

When the food supply depends upon animal food a direct analogy in the ceremonies is seen. Some Siberian tribes[†] perform a rite to increase

[*] W. H. R. Rivers, The Todas.
[†] Miss J. Harrison: Ancient Art and Ritual.

the supply of bear meat. A young bear is captured, suckled by a woman, and assumes the aspects of a sacred animal. It is finally slain in a ritual way, and the entire performance is for the purpose of increasing the supply of bear meat.

A few references may be given to indicate the views of those who have made special studies of these ceremonies. G. A. Dorsey* speaking of the Hopi tribe of the Southwest, states: "When the Hopi are not at work they are worshipping in the Kivas. The underlying element of this worship is to be found in the environment. Mother nature does not deal kindly with man in the desert. Look where you will, across the drifting sands of the plains, and the cry of man and beast is 'Water!' And so, to the gods of the rain clouds does the Hopi address his prayer. His instruments of worship are so fashioned that his magic may surpass the magic of these gods, and compel them to loosen their stores, full to overflowing. Take any one of the great Hopi ceremonies, analyze the paraphernalia worn by the

* Indians of the Southwest.

Interpretations

men, dissect the various components of the altar or sand paintings, examine the offerings made to the Spring and those placed upon the shrines, and in everything and everywhere we see prayers for rain."

Dr. Clark Wissler,[*] in speaking of primitive ceremonies, states: "One striking feature of primitive ceremonies is the elaboration of ritualistic procedure relating to the food supply. Particularly in aboriginal America we have many curious and often highly complex rituals associated with the cultivation of maize and tobacco. These often impress the student of social phenomena as extremely unusual but still highly suggestive facts, chiefly because the association seems to be between things which are wholly unrelated. Thus, among the Pawnee we find an elaborate ritual in which a few ears of maize are raised almost to the status of gods. At a certain fixed time of the autumn the official priest of this ritual proceeds with great ceremony to the fields and selects a few ears, according to

[*] The Functions of Primitive Ritualistic Ceremonies. Popular Science Monthly, August 15, 1915.

Sex Worship and Symbolism

definite standards. These are further consecrated and carefully guarded throughout the winter. At planting time the women present themselves ceremoniously to receive the seed, the necessary planting instructions, etc. Thus, it appears that during the whole year recital, there is a definite ritual in functions associated with maize culture."

The primitive tribes of Australia afford an excellent example of this type of ceremony, and fortunately these tribes have been very carefully studied. At the puberty initiations of the young men, one of the main ceremonies is a yam ceremony,* *i. e.*, a procedure to ensure a bountiful supply of the yams. A special type of yam is secured, and cooked with much ceremony under fixed rules, much care and secrecy being observed throughout. After the cooking ceremony is finished, the yams are cut up and divided among the various members of the tribe. The ceremony is supposed to increase the supply of yams. Miss

* Spencer, Native Tribes of the Northern Territory of Australia.

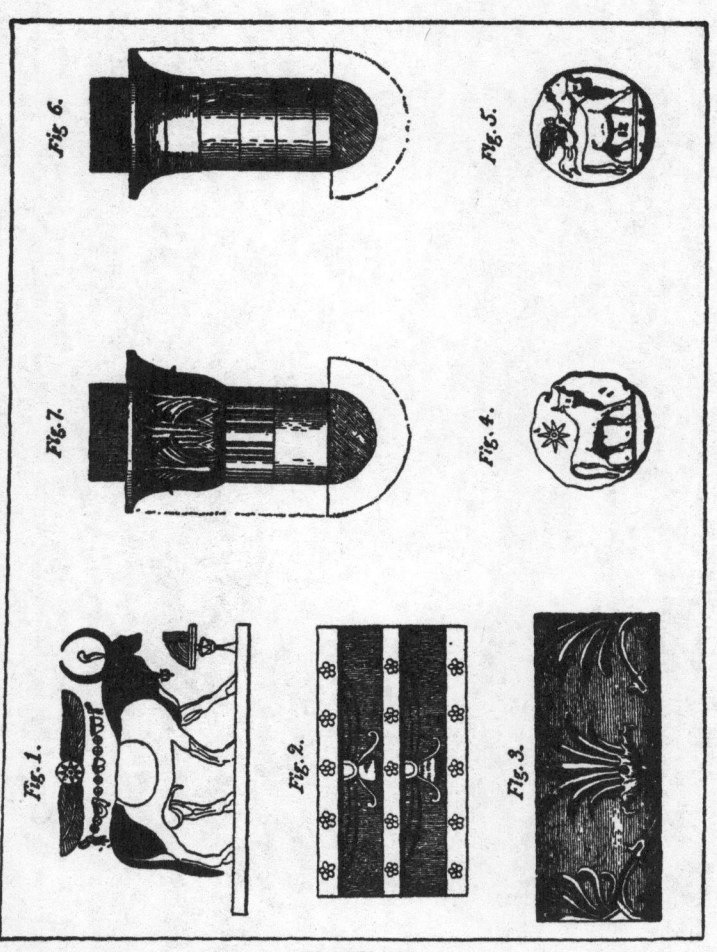

PLATE XI
EGYPTIAN FIGURES AND ORNAMENTS

Fig. 1 Symbol of sun over bull.
Fig. 2 Lotus flower design.
Fig. 3 Young shoots of lotus just when they have burst seed vessel.
Fig. 4 Sun over Taurine Bacchus.
Fig. 5 Crowning of Taurine Bacchus with wreath of laurel.
Fig. 6 Lotus seed vessel used as a capital.
Fig. 7 Same seed vessel surrounded by leaves of another plant.

Interpretations

J. Harrison* in interpreting Australian ceremonies states: "The primitive Australian takes care that magic shall not be wanting, a magic of the most instructive kind. As soon as the season of fertility approaches he begins his rites with the avowed object of making and multiplying the plants, and chiefly the animals, by which he lives; he paints the figure of the emu on the sand with vermillion drawn from his own blood; he puts on emu feathers and gazes about him in stupid fashion, like an emu bird; he makes a structure of boughs like the chrysalis of a Witchetty grub—his favorite food, and drags his body through it in pantomime, gliding and shuffling to promote its birth. Here, difficult and intricate though the ceremonies are, and uncertain in meaning as many of the details must always probably remain, the main emotional gist is clear. It is not that the Australian wonders at and admires the miracle of his Spring, the bursting of the flowers and the singing of the birds; it is not that his heart goes out in gratitude to All-Father who is the Giver of all good things;

* Ancient Art and Ritual, p. 64.

it is that, obedient to the push of life within him his impulse is towards food. He must eat that he and his tribe may grow and multiply. It is this, his will to live, that he *utters and represents.*"

In a monograph* of the Shinto religion of the Japanese, R. Hitchcock states that the leading function of the female deity is to increase the food supply. She is given the name of the Goddess of Food, or the Producer of Trees and the Parent of Grasses. She is spoken of as Abundant-Food-Lady, and seems to be a personification of the earth.

A further description of these rites is unnecessary, as wherever found they are all of the same general type. They have been described in North America, in Central Africa, in Japan, in Siberia, in India and they probably exist in many other localities. The above references indicate that they were primitive man's expression of his desire for food, this fundamental motive finding expression in an elaborate ritual.

Now since in the above rites, where the increase

* Shinto, or the Mythology of the Japanese.

Interpretations

of the food supply is the main motive, the entire development and symbolism centers about articles of food, and since in the phallic rites an entirely analagous development and symbolism centers about the generative organs, it is only reasonable to infer that the phallic rites have to do with the desire for children. In this we have the meaning of sex worship. It is primitive man's expression of his desire for the perpetuation of the race and so it represents a biological necessity, the earlier motive being for the preservation of the individual.

Fortunately the conclusions which the above arguments would appear to warrant are borne out by the statements of those who have studied these matters in great detail. Miss J. Harrison,* who also quotes Dr. Frazer, states: "The two great interests of primitive man are food and children. As Dr. Frazer has well said, if man the individual is to live he must have food; if his race is to persist he must have children, 'to live and to cause to live, to eat food and to beget children, these were the primary wants of man

* Ancient Art and Ritual.

in the past, and they will be the primary wants of men in the future so long as the world lasts.' Other things may be added to enrich and beautify human life, but, unless these wants are first satisfied, humanity itself must cease to exist. These two things, therefore, food and children, were what man chiefly sought to secure by the performance of magical rites for the regulation of the seasons. They are the very foundation stones of that ritual from which art, if we are right, took its rise."

There is a very striking parallelism between these two rites. It would be interesting to trace out these analogies step by step, but we shall refer to them only in a general way.

The outward form of the two rites is very similar. In both a religious ceremony is enacted. In the development of this ceremony a system, in which a priesthood forms a prominent part, is developed in both instances. The element of mystery runs through both procedures and, as Steven D. Peet* has stated, the nature worship

* Secret Societies and Ancient Mysteries: International Congress of Anthropology, 1893.

Interpretations

ceremony of the North American Indians bears a remarkable resemblance to the mysteries of the Eleusis and of the Bacchanalia.

In both the nature rites and the phallic rites, a sacred ceremonial object develops, and about this object a very elaborate symbolism evolves. Just as in the most primitive form of sex worship we saw that the deity consisted of a rude representation of the generative organs, so in nature worship we find that the ceremonial object is at first a rude representative of the deified animal or plant. This sacred symbol is eventually conventionalized. We have observed this in sex worship, as explained by Inman, Payne Knight and others. In the same way in nature worship, ceremonial objects are conventionalized. Spencer has shown this in the case of the Australians, the ceremonial objects eventually coming to bear a remote resemblance only to the original animal or plant representation. A. L. Kroeber[*] has observed the same development in the Arapaho Indians. The buffalo symbol for example, (a

[*] Symbolism of the Arapaho Indians: American Museum of Natural History.

very important one in this tribe since the buffalo is the chief food) has become highly conventionalized, and is finally represented by a formal rectangular design. This design now means the earth, and it is also used as a life symbol.

Again, just as we saw how in sex worship the religious symbol came to be expressed throughout decorative art, and in fact eventually became a leading motive, so it has been shown that in the nature worship of the Indians this same evolution takes place. A. L. Kroeber and Clark Wissler, among others, have shown that the decorative art on the moccasins, leggings, tents, food bags, etc., of the Indians, all representing a highly conventionalized symbol, expresses religious motives throughout. This symbolism can be interpreted only by an understanding of religious motives. The analogy of this symbolic development to that associated with sex worship is at once apparent.

Finally, just as in sex worship the motive came to dominate most of the practices and usages of civil life, so it can be shown that in tribes practicing nature worship, the religious motive has a very powerful influence. The per-

Interpretations

formance of rites to increase the food supply are among the most important of primitive man's duties. Any man who enters into these rites listlessly is not respected, and the leaders of the rite are the head men of the tribe. In Australia, one of the main functions of each Totem group is to increase the supply of its own Totem animal or plant by magic ceremony.

In summing up, therefore, the analogies between sex worship and nature worship, the following features may be reviewed: the outward form is the same, *i. e.*, that of a religious ceremonial rite in which a sacred object is the representation of the deity. The symbolism associated with this object develops in the same way in both instances. In the course of time this symbolism becomes conventionalized, and eventually it finds its way into primitive art. It then becomes the leading motive in primitive art and finally the religious motive is forgotten and the aesthetic motive alone remains. Were further proof necessary, these analogies alone would be sufficient to enable us to understand the meaning of sex worship.

Sex Worship and Symbolism

The ritual associated with the worship of sex then, arose in response to emotions which are grouped around the instinct of reproduction. These feelings are so primitive and at the same time so fundamental, that it is difficult for us to realize that early man should dignify them by religious ritual. They stand out as expressions of a biological demand. As stated above, sex worship was not a conscious expression on the part of certain individuals, but it was the unconscious expression of longings and desires on the part of the race. It represents a phase in man's mental evolution, a process of mental development. Its dynamic value, from a biological standpoint, is at once apparent. In order to survive man must reproduce his kind, and the emotions associated with reproductive instincts must be of adequate dynamic value.

It has been stated that sex worship, as practiced during the primitive state of civilization, was a healthy phase in racial evolution. In a higher degree of civilization, however, the reversion to this motive was a regression, and

Interpretations

decadent sex worship as it existed during the middle ages was an attempt by certain unhealthy elements in the race to revert to the primitive. In decadent sex worship we are dealing with an instance of faulty mental adaptation in a way in which we had not been accustomed to consider it. It is a case of faulty adaptation in the race, or at least in certain elements of it, rather than in the individual. These general analogies are noteworthy from the standpoints of mental evolution and abnormal psychology.

In order to show how sex worship as practiced by a later civilization was the expression of an unhealthy tendency, we must digress sufficiently to show the setting in which decadent sex worship existed. It is necessary to give a chronological outline indicating how primitive beliefs succeeded each other as a result of man's progressive development.

The earlier beliefs were an expression of nature worship. This as we have shown, was mostly associated with the question of food supply. It has been shown that during this period of primitive man's existence group thinking predomi-

Sex Worship and Symbolism

nated, and man thought of himself as part of the group rather than as an individual. At this time, therefore, the idea of the deity which was evolved was not that of an individual god. Generally speaking, it was the "vegetation spirit" existing throughout nature which was deified. This was the general period of earth worship,—the forces of nature associated with the earth being man's main interest. The earth at this time was highest in primitive man's regard.

During the time of earth worship, the social organization of the tribe was such that the mother was the dominating influence in social structure. Descent was matrilinear, and a society known as matriarchy existed, as contrasted to the later patriarchy. The mother was the leading figure in social as well as in family life. At this period a certain degree of sexual promiscuity existed; the mother of the child was known but the father was not and so the descent was in the female line. With earth worship, then, there was mother worship, and the term "Mother Earth" had a very real significance.

With the social state of matriarchy, the mother

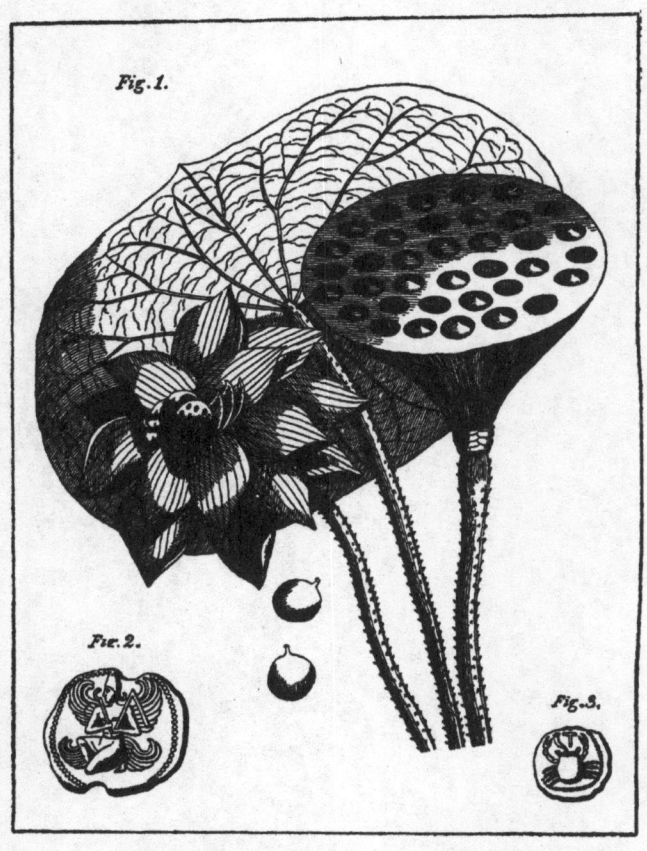

PLATE XII
THE LOTUS AND MEDALS OF MELITA

Fig. 1 Flower, leaf, and seed vessel of the lotus.
Fig. 2 Generative spirit with wings like Jewish Cherubim brooding over matter.
Fig. 3 The crab as the symbol of the productive powers of the waters.

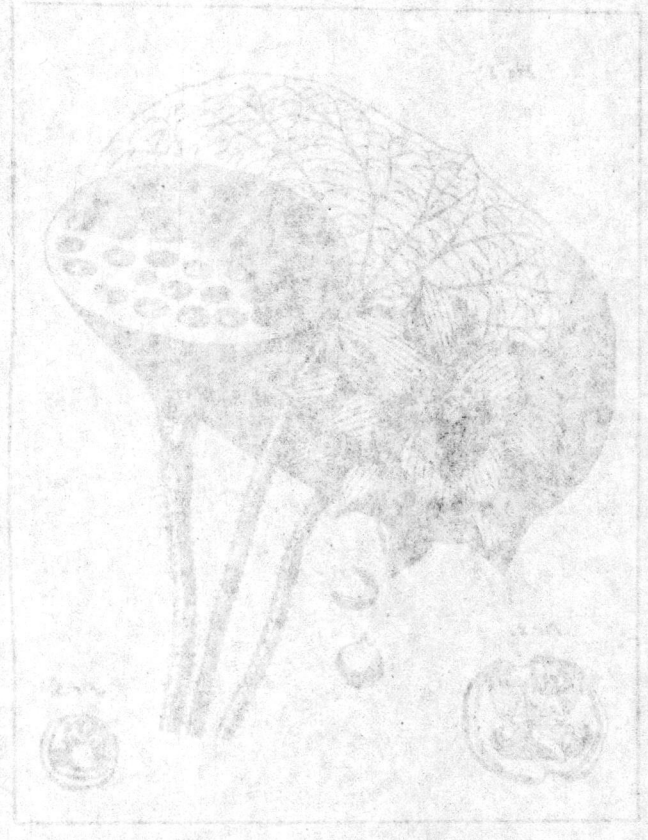

Interpretations

cults developed. These mother cults evolved the numerous female deities of antiquity, Themis, Demeter, Cybele, and many others being the expression of mother worship. These deities were generally associated with the wild elements of nature,—with the wind, and the hills and the forests.

Associated with the mother religion in a way which at first does not appear to be very clear arose the phallic cults. It should be here stated that the mother religion was not the religion of the mother alone, but also that of the mother and child. The child was the adolescent,—a youth about to be initiated at the public ceremony, at which he was often circumcised and after which he was able to take up the reproductive functions of the male. Miss J. Harrison has shown that Dionysus was the embodiment of this conception. Here the youth was necessary only to the extent that he could become a father. It was his generative attribute which was sanctified, rather than that he was a male being existing as an individual. For this reason, the deification of the phallic principle, *i. e.*, the generative

Sex Worship and Symbolism

attribute, preceded the deification of the male as an individual. At least this is the impression one gains of this development. In any case, we note that the phallic ceremonies were associated with the mother religion. The period in which both existed was mostly prehistoric.

We see the beginning of the evolution of the male god in the phallic cults. This was eventually followed by the patriarchal system and here we are on more familiar ground. Patriarchy succeeded matriarchy, but whether as a gradual evolution or otherwise is not clear. Some writers speak of bitter conflicts in Persia, India, Greece and elsewhere. In any case the religion of the father replaced that of the mother; the social system changed and the father took his place at the head of the family. During this period we are told[*] that man shifted his belief from the earth to the sky, the sun was found to be the source of energy and the worship was transferred to the Heavens. Just as formerly the female deity was identified with the earth, so the male deity was identified with the sun,

[*] Miss J. Harrison, Themis, Introduction.

Interpretations

Zeus and Apollo being two examples of the latter type from a great many.

We are now approaching a well known historic period. The religion of the father and the son had replaced that of the mother and child. The age of hero worship has commenced and this hero was often identified with the sun. For this reason, the fact that a myth is in the form of a sun myth does not argue against its being the expression of a very deep religious motive. As has been stated, earlier motives are carried forward, and so while sun worship is a somewhat later development than the phallic beliefs, it is quite natural than many phallic ideas should find expression at this subsequent period.

We have now reached a time when sex worship became decadent, for Christianity followed sun worship and hero worship; and this brings us to the present day. The religion of father and son remains, and much of the form of the earlier worship has been retained in the modern.

The above outline of the changes and evolution of early religions is most schematic. It enables us, however, to see that sex worship was entirely

Sex Worship and Symbolism

out of place during the middle ages, in a civilization which had long before discarded matriarchy. The questions of the food supply, and of children, were no longer so immediately pressing, and the faith in magical performances had been shaken. Man had emerged from the group as a definite personality, and the development of a new religion which expressed other feelings and desires had taken place. What we wish to emphasize at present is, then, that sex worship as it was carried on during the middle ages was a distinctly unnatural tendency in the race.

At this time opportunity may be taken to reconcile different interpretations which some writers have given regarding early religious motives. Considerable variation and some contradiction may be observed in the writings of different authors in describing a religious development of much the same period. One writer may describe the features of nature worship and quite ignore the presence of sex worship. Others may describe only phallic rites. These discrepancies may be understood when the order in which the various beliefs developed is recognized.

Interpretations

Nature worship developed first, but much of its symbolism was carried into the phallic ceremonies. Thus we see the phallus associated with the pine cone and other elements of vegetative life. Some of these elements, the pine cone for example, finally came to have a phallic significance, but at an earlier period they probably represented the vegetation spirit. In fact, reproductive attributes of both nature and man were often worshipped at the same ceremony.

While we should not as a rule expect to find phallic rites associated with the earlier forms of nature worship, since sex worship developed at a somewhat later period, still in this connection we cannot be too dogmatic; the primitive Australians appear to be at the stage of mental development when simple nature worship predominated, yet, from *Mutter Erde** we learn that with the Australians a ceremony consisting of the throwing of a spear into the earth was of phallic significance. This co-existence of these two related motives is not unnatural since they

* A. Dieterich: Mutter Erde.

both equally represent fundamental biological demands on the part of the race.

We may now return to the interpretation of decadent sex worship. When we understand the setting in which sex worship was practiced in the middle ages we are better able to appreciate its significance. As stated above, it was the attempt by certain elements of the race to return to more primitive motives, and to derive satisfaction from beliefs which had long been outgrown by advancing civilization. This clinging to an early type of reaction, or the return to more primitive feelings, must be regarded as an unhealthy tendency. Moreover, at this time, the motive itself was no longer expressed in the natural and healthy way of primitive times. Sex worship during the middle ages became depraved; excesses and perversions appeared and the entire development, as it existed at that time, was biologically undesirable.

It also appeared that at certain times in the mental evolution of the race a degree of development is reached from which no further progress is made. At least, we are aware of such an

Interpretations

instance in the case of a very primitive community in Southern Italy. A writer, Norman Douglas,* in 1914 found the existence of a phallic cult in Calabria. The women sanctified a crack of one of the walls of the temple, their attitude toward it corresponding to the yoni worship of India. Near by was an ancient stone pillar held in great veneration, which was the representative of the phallus.

It is observed that in this small community some remnants of phallic belief of a very primitive type have been retained for centuries. The religious development, an index of mental development, has become "set" as it were and no further progress is possible. It is not entirely for want of opportunity that this locality has not taken up higher religious beliefs. The Catholic Church has introduced its teachings, but the people have represented the images of the Saints, of the Virgin Mary, and of Christ somewhat after the fashion of toy dolls. These are used as fetishes to ward off disease and no higher conceptions are grasped. Ideas regarding

* Norman Douglas: Old Calabria.

after life and immortality are disregarded in favor of the immediate need of protection against supposed evil influences. With these people, therefore, motives are utilized which satisfy only the most fundamental and immediate desires.

We have now followed a definite motive in mental development through its rise, its elaboration and its decadence. We therefore have its life history in the race before us; we have been enabled by analogies of other motives and by utilizing the conclusions of various writers, to understand its meaning and to give its interpretation. It remains to be seen what general conclusions regarding either racial or individual development in this sphere may be drawn.

It appears that when an important motive of this sort develops in the race, it embodies the expression of fundamental desires. Since it carries with it a strong and ever present desire in this way, it is strikingly *dynamic* in nature. It dominates all social organization, and with primitive people it dominates much of the conduct of the individual. When such a motive is

Interpretations

seriously entertained it is pragmatic, *i. e.,* it serves a useful end, or at least the conceptions which it embodies are entertained because they are thought to be of the highest value to the race.

As mental development continues, these more fundamental and primitive motives cease to be all absorbing. Eventually, the subject of the food supply becomes less pressing. Races continue to increase and multiply with or without the performance of sacred rites and man begins to question the utility of his imitative magic. Higher desires force themselves into consciousness, and earlier motives are no longer outwardly expressed; the form of the early motives is retained, however: usages, symbols and practices which have long ceased to be dynamic and whose meaning is entirely forgotten are still observed; so we see evidences of primitive racial motives cropping up in all sorts of ways in later civilization.

But to say that the earlier motives are no longer outwardly expressed is not to infer that they do not exist. Fundamental as they are in our mental development, they enter into our

Sex Worship and Symbolism

general personality and become a part of our makeup. How is the motive expressed in sex worship a part of our motives and feelings of today? Superficially it does not appear to be present, but a little reflection shows that it is there. It has become so much a part of us that we scarcely recognize its presence, the instinct to reproduce being common to everyone. Every woman feels this to be her duty,—her religious duty if the dictum of the Church is to be followed:

"Lo, children are an heritage of the Lord; and the fruit of the womb is his reward. As arrows are in the hand of a mighty man; so are children of the youth. Happy is the man that has his quiver full of them; they shall not be ashamed, but they shall speak with the enemies in the gate." *Psalm 127.*

During earlier times barrenness was regarded as a curse, and many charms were in use to counteract this calamity. A sentence from a letter of Julia Ward Howe to her young sister about to be married, affords an apt reference to this sense of duty: "Marriage, like death, is a

PLATE XIII
BACCHUS AND MEDALS OF CAMARINA AND SYRACUSE

Fig. 1 Incubation of the vital spirit represented by a serpent wreathed around an egg.
Fig. 2 Oriental symbol of sun (disc with wings)
Fig. 3 Sun fructifying the waters represented by swan.
Fig. 4 Victory mounting chariot of sun.
Fig. 5 Victory flying before chariot of sun.
Fig. 6 Asterisk in place of victory.
Fig. 7 The vine between the creating deity (Bacchus) and the destroying deity represented by the tiger.

Interpretations

debt we owe to nature, and though it costs us something to pay it, yet we are more content and better established in peace when we have paid it." The feeling associated with the command "to increase and multiply" is so much a part of our innermost thoughts and feelings that further references to it are unnecessary.

To what extent may we utilize the evolution of this motive in the race, in understanding certain phases of mental development associated with reproductive instincts in the individual? In interpreting the racial history of this motive we have seen that it is dynamic; it develops in response to biological demands. It is a very elementary and primitive desire to be raised to the dignity of a religion, but none the less it is a very essential one. We have seen that when this motive is replaced by higher ones, a return to it bespoke faulty mental adaptations on the part of those who did so. Analogies between the individual and the race in this sphere exist in a general way, and their presence is significant.

Analogies in the sphere in the normal mental development of the individual may be considered first. In dealing with the developing thoughts of childhood, we shall refer to one particular tendency, *i. e.*, that of *day dreaming*. We know that a certain amount of the day dreaming of the child has to do with the feelings and emotions associated with the questions of reproduction, considered in its broadest sense; *i. e.*, including fictitious lovers, marriages, children, etc. Now probably with the child, the day dreaming associated with these feelings is of biological significance, just as the rituals associated with similar feeelings are of value to the race. The little girl who is the mother of her doll, who plays at housekeeeping, who fictitiously assumes the responsibilities of married life and what not, —the child by developing this feature of her existence in fancy is probably preparing herself for reality. The little boy who becomes a hero in his own fancy, marries a princess, and who overcomes all sorts of difficulties; or the small boy who in his play enters into all the activities of adult life,—probably this child, by entertaining the thoughts of his future life, prepares himself to some extent for future life. These

Interpretations

fundamental motives, therefore, which arise in response to biological demands, are the expression of desires, both in the case of the individual and of the race, and they act not only harmlessly but probably beneficially at a certain stage of mental evolution.

Again, we have shown how in the race remnants of early primitive motives continue to appear in various ways long after their outward dynamic value has been lost and when their meaning is no longer understood. Is this not true of the individual? Do we not all recognize in the moods and mental attributes and even in some of the actions of the adult, remnants of feelings and forces which were dynamic in childhood? These feelings exist although they are not consciously appreciated. The actual experiences are forgotten but the moods and emotions remain. This is analagous to the influence which primitive racial thoughts, beliefs and usages have on present day civilization. The meaning of these usages and symbols is forgotten in many cases but the outward form still exists.

In the individual, a motive of this kind does

not become a religion or a ritual as in the case with the race, but it nevertheless is forcefully expressed in that it excites an absorbing interest and forces itself strongly into consciousness, during the phase of its dynamic development. As stated above, just as in the early mental evolution of the race, we find that the question of reproduction comes prominently to the fore, so with the individual we find that at the adolescent period of life the sexual instinct is very fully elaborated. Just as with the race reproduction is necessary for the continuation of the race, so with the individual, elaboration of sexual instinct is necessary in order that adult sexual responsibilities may be assumed. This consists of much more than mere physical development. In a complex state of civilization many adjustments in the sphere of sexual indulgence and continence and marriage have to be made. This phase of the individual's life is a very important one. It is the rule for proper reactions to occur at this time, in which case the reproductive instincts assume their proper place in mental life. But if satisfactory adjustments do not

Interpretations

occur the consequences may be serious. In the healthy mental evolution of the individual, therefore, just as in the normal mental evolution of the race, we see that motives arise, assume a dynamic character, play their part in the developing mind, and leave lasting impressions. They serve a useful purpose during one phase of mental evolution. We have seen that they may be harmful in the race if utilized at a later period. Let us see to what extent this is true of the individual.

Psychiatrists during recent years have come to believe that in certain mental states we see a reversion to a more primitive type of reaction, —a tendency to utilize earlier adaptations, the reactions of infancy and childhood in meeting situations which arise in adult life. If this assumption is correct it is seen that a reversion to something more primitive is an undesirable reaction in the individual as well as in the race. Here too we find that the emotions and feelings associated with the reproductive instinct may be inadequately developed. It has been shown above that the day dreams of the child are probably beneficial rather than harmful. Is this day dreaming beneficial to the adult? We know from our experience that it is not, and in its relation to the reproductive sphere this is particularly true. The adult who substitutes the realities of life by elaborate day dreams is approaching dangerous ground. The young woman who in adult life is constantly dreaming of an ideal but fictitious lover is deriving satisfaction from unhealthy sources; and the young man who ecstatically becomes a hero or a racial benefactor is equally at fault. In instances where such thoughts are believed in and acted upon as we observe again and again in mental disorders, a serious condition of the mind has arisen. When an attempt is made to gain satisfaction in these immature ways at a later stage of development, or when there is a failure to develop at a certain point, the reaction is harmful in both the individual and in the race.

It is during the adolescent period that these failures of adaptation generally occur. At this time, the whole development in the reproductive

Interpretations

sphere, particularly in the mental characteristics associated with the sexual instinct, considered in its broadest sense, does not take place. There may be much rumination about this topic, but the responsibilities of adult sexual life, of marriage, of child bearing with the female, are not adequately met. Fancies are substituted for reality, and while, as stated above, young women may dream of ideal lovers, they at the same time are shy and unnatural in their attitude toward the opposite sex. Young men, instead of taking their place in the life of the adult community, realize adult ambitions only by elaborate day dreams. In abnormal mental states, we see young men in their fancies become important personages, religious benefactors and national heroes. They may shun all association with women but at the same time maintain that they have a cultural mission to populate the earth. We see here how the feelings associated with reproductive instincts have been faulty or inadequate. This return to something more primitive is an unhealthy atavistic tendency and makes for both racial and individual inferiority.

Sex Worship and Symbolism

A word may be said regarding symbolism of the race as applied to the individual. We have stated that symbolism is a primitive and rudimentary way of expressing thought. It would seem logical therefore that if in some abnormal mental states there is a return to more primitive reactions, we may find a tendency to symbolize. This tendency is frequently observed and the symbolism is often very elaborate. A knowledge of the interpretation of racial symbolism is doubtless of value in the case of the individual. When men's thoughts deal with the same subject and when they tend to symbolize, they are likely to express themselves in much the same way symbolically. If in abnormal mental states thoughts are entertained which have to do with the motives we have been discussing, it is reasonable to suppose that the racial and individual symbolism will show certain analogies.

Again, in the pages of recent psychiatry, we learn that in abnormal mental states there is a reversion not only to the primitive motives of childhood, but also to the primitive motives of the race. Just to what extent this tendency

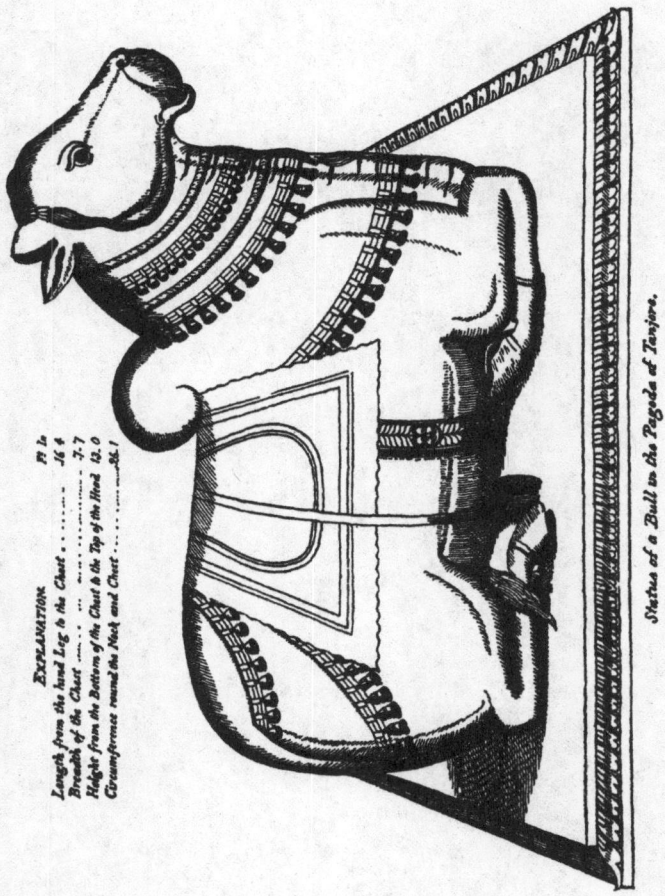

PLATE XIV
STATUE OF A BULL IN THE PAGODA OF TANJORE

Interpretations

exists remains for studies of the future to show. Certainly, striking instances may be cited; for example, let us quote from a recent study in psychiatry:* "One such patient with a very complicated delusional system states that he is the father of Adam, that he has lived in his present human body thirty-five years, but in other bodies thirty million years, and that during this time he has occupied six million different bodies. He has been the great men in the history in the development of the human race; he himself created the human race. It took him three hundred million years to perfect the first fully developed human being; he is both male and female and identifies all the different parts of the Universe with his own body; heaven, hell and purgatory are located in his limbs, the stars are pieces of his body which had been torn apart by torture and persecution in various ages of past history; he is the father and creator of the various races and elements of the human organization, etc." Any one who has done even a

* Jelliffe and White, Diseases of the Nervous System, page 689.

Sex Worship and Symbolism

cursory reading in mythology cannot but be struck by the similarity in form as well as in thought between this production and what we find in myths.

The general analogies which we have indicated are such as one would have reason to expect. The history of both the healthy and unhealthy evolution of the race is in many respects the history of the individual; in order to understand these analogies it is necessary to understand the mental development of primitive man. Recent studies have given us much valuable information in this direction. In primitive usages we find the expression of early man's deepest longings and desires, and so a dynamic interpretation of such motives is possible. It remains for the psychiatrist to learn to what extent the findings of special investigators of primitive races may be utilized in explaining mental evolution, and also the development of abnormal mental states. This study is a comparatively recent one but it already gives indications of offering ample rewards.

REFERENCES AND BIBLIOGRAPHY

REFERENCES AND BIBLIOGRAPHY

Brand, John: Observations on Popular Antiquities.

Bryant: System of Mythology.

Cox, Rev. G. W.: The Mythology of the Aryan Nations.

DeGubertnatis, Angelo: Zoological Mythology.

Deiterich, A.: Mutter Erde.

Dixon, Roland B.: The Northern Maidu.

Dorsey, George A.: Traditions of the Caddo, (Carnegie Institute.) Indians of the South West.

Frazer, J. G.: Adonis, Attis and Osiris; Balder, the Beautiful; Psyche's Task.

Goodrich, V. K.: Ainu Family Life and Religion, Popular Science Monthly, November, 1888.

Grosse: The Beginnings of Art.

Harrison, Miss Jane: Ancient Art and Ritual; Themis.

Hearn, Lafcadio: Japan; an Attempt at Interpretation.

Herodotus: (Rawlinson's Trans.)

Higgins, Godfrey: The Anacalypsis; Celtic Druids.

Hitchcock, Romyn: Shinto or the Mythology of the Japanese, (Smithsonian Institute.)

Howitt, A. W.: The Native Tribes of South East Australia.

Jennings, Hargrave: The Rosicrucians; The Indian Religions.

Jevons, F. B.: The Idea of God in Early Religions.

Judson: Myths and Legends of the Mississippi Valley and the Great Lakes.

Karpas, Morris J.: Socrates in the light of Modern Psychopathology. (Journal of Abnormal Psychology. 1915.)

King, C. W.: The Gnostics and their Remains; Hand-book of Engraved Gems.

Knight, R. P.: The Symbolical Language of Ancient Art and Mythology; Two Essays on the Worship of Priapus.

Kroeber, Alfred L.: Symbolism of the Arapaho Indians. The Arapaho, (Bulletin of the American Museum of Natural History.)

Langdon, S.: Tammuz and Ishtar.

References and Bibliography

Layard, A.: Babylon and Nineveh; Nineveh and its Remains.

Leuba, James H.: A Psychological Study of Religion.

Monsen, Frederick: Festivals of the Hopi. (The Craftsman, June, 1907.)

Murray, Gilbert: Hamlet and Orestes: The Rise of the Greek Epic.

Newton, John: Assyrian Grove Worship.

O'Brien, Henry: The Round Towers of Ireland.

Peet, Stephen D.: Secret Societies and Sacred Mysteries.

Perrot and Chipiez: History of Art in Phrygia, Lidia, Caria and Lycia; History of Art in Persia.

Prescott: Conquest of Peru.

Pratt, J. B.: India and Its Faiths.

Rawlinson, G.: History of Ancient Egypt; Ancient Monarchies.

Reclus, Elie: Primitive Folk.

Rivers, W. H. R.: The Todas.

Rhyn, Dr. Otto: Mysteria.

Roscoe, John: The Northern Bantu.

Rocco, Sha: Ancient Sex Worship.

Rousselet, Louis: India and Its Native Princes.

Sex Worship and Symbolism

Spencer, B.: Native Tribes of the Northern Territory of Australia.

Solas, W. J.: Ancient Hunters.

Starcke, C. V.: The Primitive Family.

Stevens, J.: Central America, Chiapez and Yucatan.

Symonds, J. A.: A Problem in Greek Ethics.

Wissler, Clark: Symbolism in the Decorative Art of the Sioux.

Westropp, Hodder M.: Primitive Symbolism.

Wood, Rev. J. G.: The Uncivilized Races.

Wood-Martin: Pagan Ireland.

INDEX

INDEX

Adaptations, faulty, 131-132.
Adjustment, of individual, 130.
Adonis, sun god, 77.
American Cyclopedia, 23.
American Museum of Natural History, 7.
Anacalipsis, 39.
Analogies between the Individual and the Race, 127.
Ancient Grove Worship of Assyria, 49, 73.
Ancient Sex Worship, 25, 30, 42.
Androgyne deity, 38, 67.
Arapaho Indians, 111.

Bacchus, representative of male generative attribute, 22.
Bacchanalia, 76, 80, 88, 111.
Bear, sacred animal, 104.
Bull, phallic significance of, 63.
Bull roarer, nature of, 102.

Bureau of Amer. Eth., 7.

Caves of Elephanta, 44.
Ceremonial objects, conventionalization of, 111.
Chinese Review, 45.
Collective or group feeling, importance of, 21.
Collective thought of the race, relation to religious development, 17.
Crux Ansata, 51.

Dairy, sacredness of, 103.
Dances, at Witches' Sabbath, 90.
Decadent Sex Worship, 81, 83, 93, 115; interpretation of, 122.
Deity, female, function of in Japan, 108.
Deities, Teutonic, 94.
Dietrich, A., 121.
Dionysia, 76, 80.
Dionysus, 117.
Dorsey, G. A., 104.
Douglas, N., 123.
Dragon, relation to serpent, 45.

Index

Earth, Worship, 116.
Egg, 51, 62, 75.
Eleusenia, 76, 79, 89, 110.
Emasculation, a form of worship, 30.
Essay on the Assyrian "Grove," 40.

Female deities, 117.
Festivals to increase food supply, 101.
Fire, male principle, 37.
Fire Worship, 37, 90; identified with sex worship, 43.
Fish, phallic significance, 36.
Frazer, 7, 17, 30, 31, 95, 109.

Gnostics, early secret society, 84; phallic amulets of, 91; reversions of, 85.
Goat, priapic animal, 89; Symbol of Khem, 25.
Golden Bough, 7. (See Frazer.)
Group Thought, 116.

Harrison, J., 8, 18, 102, 103, 107, 109, 117, 118.
Hearn, L., 52.

Heraldry, origin of symbols, 51.
Hermes, phallic nature of, 37.
Higgins, 39.
Hitchcock, R., 108.
Holy Grail, Symbolism of, 94.
Homosexuality, in Greek life, 86; practice of Rosicrucians, 85.
Hopi Indians, 104.
Howe, J. W., 126.
Howitt, A. W., 8.

Initiative magic, 106.
India and its Native Princes, 44.
India and its Faiths, 81.
Indian Religions, 49.
Indians of the Southwest, 104.
Infantile reactions, 131.
Initiation ceremony, 117.
Inman, T., 7, 51, 54.
Interpretations of Sex Worship, 99.

Japan, an attempt at Interpretation, 52.
Jennings, H., 7, 27, 42, 49, 51, 62, 74, 93.

Index

Karnac, 26.
Karpas, M. J., 86.
Khem, description of, 24.
King, C. W., 54.
Knight, R. P., 7, 27, 29, 38, 48, 49, 50, 54, 58, 63, 64, 84, 88, 91, 92.
Knights of the Round Table, 93.
Knights Templar, phallic amulets of, 91; practices of, 87.
Kroebler, A. L., 111, 112.

Layard, A., 60.
Lingam with yoni, 41.
Lost god, the, 77.
Lotus, significance of, 56-58.

Male date palm, significance of, 49.
Matriarchy, 116.
May-pole, associated with phallic worship, 39, 48.
Moon, associated with female deity, 72.
Mother Earth, 72, 116.
Mother religion, 117, 118.
Mutter Erde, 121.
Murray, G., 20.
Mysteries, teaching of, 79, 80.

Nature Worship, 7, 100, 110, 112.
Newton, J., 40, 49, 73.
Nineveh and Its Remains, 60.
North American Indians and sun worship, 71; nature worship, 101, 111, 112.

Obelisk, phallic interpretation, 38.
O'Brien, 39, 56, 58.
Obscure Sex Symbolism, 37.
Order of the Garter, 94.
Osiris, 77.

Pan, significance of, 22.
Patriarchy, 116, 118.
Pepys, S., 48.
Peet, O. S., 110.
Persephone, 79.
Phallic hand, symbol of prostitution, 92.
Phallic rites, motive for, 109.
Phallic symbols, 26; in art, 51.
Phallic Worship in China, 45.
Phallic Worship, nature of, 23, 101.

Index

Phallus, as a charm, 91, 94; as a decoration, 91.
Plant and Flower Symbols 54.
Pomegranate, as a female symbol, 56.
Pratt, J. B., 81.
Priapiea, 88.
Priapus, disguises of, 89.
Primitive motives, continuance of, 129; reversion to, 134.
Primitive Symbolism, 28.
Problem in Greek Ethics, 86.
Psyche's Task, 95.
Puberity Initiations, 106, 117.

Qualities of animal and vegetable nature venerated, 40.

Racial feelings, expression of, in religion, 19.
Racial Motives, in primitive religions, 19; dynamic value of, 125.
Rain making rite, 100.
Rawlinson, 23.
Reproduction, motive of, 21.

Rhyn, O., 79.
Rise of the Greek Epic, 20.
Ritual, motive for, 107; related to food supply, 105, 106.
Rivers, W. H. R., 6, 103.
Robin Goodfellow, 95.
Rosicrucians, 43, 93.
Rosicrucians, phallic amulets of, 91; practices of, 85, 86, 93.
Round Towers of Ireland, 39, 74.
Rousselet, 44.

Sacred Animals, 60-65.
Sacred prostitution, evidences of, 29.
Satan, at Witches' Sabbath, 89.
Secret Societies for decadent sex worship, 84.
Serpent Worship, 61, 62, 74, 75.
Sex Worship:
  An unconscious racial expression, 21; biological significance of, 99; as basis of early religions, 28; In Africa in Modern times, 26;

Index

decadence of in Middle Ages, 90; primitive form, 111; influence in present thought, 126; part of evolution of the human mind, 23; in symbolism, 35; where it existed as basis of early religions, 28.
Sex Worship and Nature Worship, analogies of, 113; relation of, 121.
Sexual act, as part of worship, 27-28.
Shinto, or the mythology of the Japanese, 108.
Smithsonian Inst., 7.
Snake, phallic significance of, 36.
Socrates in the light of Modern Psychopathology, 86.
Spencer, 8.
Star and crescent, 54.
Stonehenge, significance of, 39, 71.
Sun Myth, 119.
Sun Worship, 37, 71, 74, 75.
Symbolic Language of Ancient Art and Mythology, 50, 59.

Symbolism, racial, in the individual, 134.
Symonds, J. A., 86.

Themis, 8, 102, 118.
Thunder god, 102.
Thunder rites, 102.
Todas, the, 6, 103.
Totem, 112.
Tree Worship, 49.

Upright objects as phalli, 38.

Vegetation spirit, 116.

Water, female principle, 37.
Weathercock, emblem of the sun, 50.
Westropp, H. M., 28, 46, 55.
Wilder, A., 59.
Witchcraft, 93.
Witches' Sabbath, nature of, 90, 92.
Wissler, C., 105, 112.
Worship of Priapus, 49, 84, 88, 92.

Yam ceremony, 106.